Excel 2024 for Beginners

EXCEL 2024 ESSENTIALS - BOOK 1

M.L. HUMPHREY

SELECT TITLES BY M.L. HUMPHREY

EXCEL 2024 ESSENTIALS
Excel 2024 for Beginners
Intermediate Excel 2024
Excel 2024 Useful Functions

EXCEL 365 ESSENTIALS
Excel 365 for Beginners
Intermediate Excel 365
102 Useful Excel 365 Functions

EXCEL ESSENTIALS 2019
Excel 2019 Beginner
Excel 2019 Intermediate
Excel 2019 Formulas & Functions

EXCEL ESSENTIALS
Excel for Beginners
Intermediate Excel
50 Useful Excel Functions
50 More Excel Functions

WORD ESSENTIALS
Word for Beginners
Intermediate Word

POWERPOINT ESSENTIALS
PowerPoint for Beginners
Intermediate PowerPoint

ACCESS ESSENTIALS
Access for Beginners
Intermediate Access

See mlhumphrey.com for all titles by M.L. Humphrey

CONTENTS

Introduction

Excel is one of the most powerful software programs for a normal every day user. I would be lost without it at work and I'm not quite sure how I'd keep track of monthly bills without it. (Probably in the margin of a notebook like I used to in the old days.)

But it can be really intimidating for a new user to learn. Especially if you pick up a book that's trying to cover everything you can possibly know in Excel. Because the program can do SO MUCH. This is my fourth time writing a series of books on Excel, and I'd say each time I cover maybe 30% of all the possible things that Excel can do. And yet the collection still ends up being an inch thick in print.

Good news, though, by the time you're done with this first book in the series, I think you'll know about 90-95% of what you need to know to use Excel on a daily basis, and you'll have a good idea of how to learn the rest.

My goal is to give you what you need to know without bogging you down in a lot of stuff you don't need to know. *Intermediate Excel 2024* and *Excel 2024 Useful Functions*, which are the next two books in this series, will keep you going if you want to learn more. But by the time you're done with this book you should feel comfortable opening Excel, entering and moving data around, formatting it, doing some basic analysis, and printing your results.

I want to show you that Excel does not have to be scary, and that anyone can learn it.

Now, that does mean I start with the basics of all basics and cover things like terminology, opening Excel, starting a new file, saving in Excel, etc. For those who already know that, I think there's still value to be had here. We'll cover sorting, filtering, and basic formulas, too. But you can also just jump ahead to the other titles in the series. That's why there are multiple titles. So people can jump in where they need to.

(And if you have some experience and want a little taste of how I teach, check out *Excel Tips and Tricks* which should be free in ebook and provides some simple time-saving tricks I've learned over the years.)

One more thing to note before we get started. This book is written for users of Excel 2024.

At the beginner level, most of what you learn here can be used in any version of Excel. What differentiates this book and the original Excel title I wrote, *Excel for Beginners*, is that I'm not going to hold back on telling you new ways of doing things that are available in Excel 2024 but weren't in earlier versions of Excel.

Again, at the beginner level there's not too much of that. But if you continue with this series then things like pivot charts and the newer functions will be something you can use in Excel 2024 (or Excel 365) but not in earlier versions of Excel. That backwards compatibility issue is probably less of a concern these days than it was back in the day, but I once wasted a week using a function that was available in my version of Excel only to figure out it wasn't available to my consulting client and had to redo everything as a result. Not fun.

Anyway. Your big difference as a beginner in Excel will be the appearance of Excel 2024 versus earlier editions. It seems with each release they like to streamline things more and more so that they are less visually intuitive. Fine for someone like me who has been using variations of Excel for over 30 years, not so great for a new user.

Also, know that my screenshots may look slightly different from what you see on your screen. That's because the section at the top of Excel will display differently depending on the screen size of the computer you're on. Also there are various appearance settings that can impact how Excel looks. Things should always be in the same location, though, so if you get lost look for the little image (the icon) for each option, or for a dropdown menu with that section name.

Finally, I print these books in black and white to make them as affordable for readers as possible, but sometimes it is nice to see color images. The ebook versions of these books are in color and if you go to the About the Author section at the end of this book there is a discount code for buying the ebook off of my Payhip store.

Okay. First up, basic terminology.

Terminology

This chapter includes terms that I'm going to use throughout the rest of the book and also starts some of your basic learning. So even if you think you know Excel, be sure to skim it just in case.

Workbook

A workbook is basically an Excel file.

Workbooks are made up of worksheets. While the default for a workbook in Excel 2024 is to have one worksheet, you can easily add more.

Worksheet

According to Microsoft, a worksheet is "the primary document that you use in Excel to store and work with data." Worksheets consist of "cells that are organized into columns and rows".

That is the official definition, but in more recent versions of Excel I have seen worksheets that did not have columns and rows. They were simply blank pages that could display an image. So the better way to think of a worksheet is as a discrete location in your workbook that contains information. (We will not deal with any situations that involve those blank pages, though, so feel free to forget that for now.)

Note that the Office folks also sometimes refer to a worksheet as a spreadsheet. I don't, because to me that can also mean a workbook.

Cell

Cells are formed by the intersection of a column and a row, and are referred to based upon the column and row where they are located.

So the first cell in a worksheet is Cell A1, where A is the first column and 1 is the first row. When a cell is selected, you can see a border around the edge of the cell, like here where Cell A1 is selected:

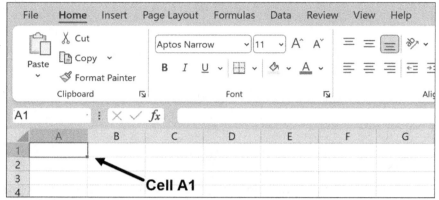

Cell A1

When you enter information into a worksheet, it is almost always entered into a specific cell. You can then refer to that cell to use that information.

Cells generally will contain text, numeric values, or formulas.

Column

A standard worksheet uses columns and rows to create cells which display your information. Columns run across the top of the worksheet and are, by default, indicated with a letter. Here is the top left corner of a worksheet:

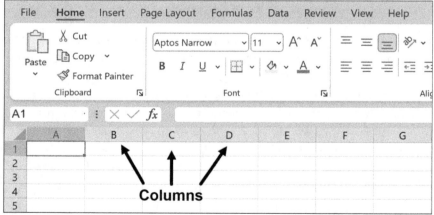

Columns

See the letters running across the top there? A, B, C, D, etc.? Each of those letters is at the top of a column.

Every Excel 2024 worksheet has the exact same number of columns. Scroll far enough to the right and the columns will start a double alphabet of AA, AB, AC, etc. This will continue into a triple alphabet AAA, AAB, etc. The very last column in an Excel 2024 worksheet is XFD.

Row

Rows run down the side of a worksheet and are numbered from 1 up to the very last row, which in Excel 2024 is 1,048,576.

Here is that image above but with the rows pointed out instead:

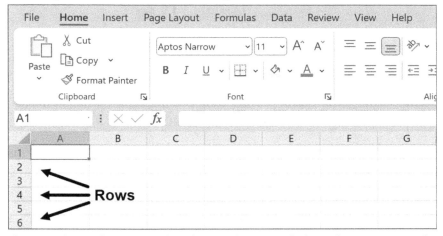

(Note that the number of rows and columns in a worksheet is one area where different versions of Excel can be incompatible. I wrote the first Excel book in Office 2013. In that version, the maximum number of rows was 65,536. You cannot take data that fills all of the rows in a worksheet in Excel 2024 and transfer it to a worksheet in Excel 2013. It wouldn't fit.)

Click

You probably already click on things all the time without thinking about it, but just in case.

If I tell you to click on something, that means to use your mouse (or trackpad) to move the arrow on the screen to a specific location, and then to left-click or right-click (as defined below).

In general, a left-click will select an item whereas a right-click will create a dropdown list of options to choose from. If I don't tell you which one to use, left-click.

Left-Click/Right-Click

If you use a standard mouse, then it's going to be split in the middle with the option to press down on either side. Press on the left side and that's a left-click. Press on the right side and that's a right-click.

With trackpads it can be a little trickier, because they sometimes get creative about where they put things. On my current computer I can left-click on my trackpad by either clicking on a flat button at the *top* of the trackpad or by pressing in the bottom left corner. Right-click also has two options, a visible button at the top right and pressing in the bottom right corner of the trackpad itself.

If you're not sure how to left- or right-click on your computer, experiment a bit. I will mention times to use one or the other throughout this book that you can use as your test cases.

Left-Click and Drag

I may at times tell you to left-click and drag something. What this means is to left-click on that object or in that location, and then hold your left-click as you move your arrow/mouse/cursor to either select a range or to move an object.

Formula Bar

The formula bar is the long white bar at the top of the Excel workspace with the function(x) *fx* symbol next to it.

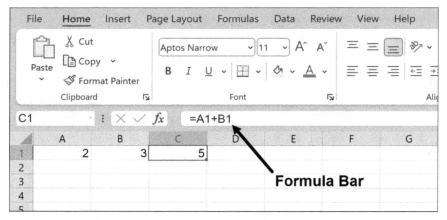

When you click onto a cell, like I have here in Cell C1, the formula bar will show you the contents of that selected cell. If the contents of the cell are just text or numbers you typed in, that's what you'll see. But if a formula was used instead, the formula bar will display the formula that was used.

This is useful because by default the cells in a worksheet only display the results of any formulas that were used.

Above, for example, I used a formula in Cell C1 that adds the value in Cell A1 to the value in Cell B1. You can see the result of the formula, 5, in Cell C1, and the formula used, =A1+B1, in the formula bar.

Tab

I refer to the menu choices at the top of the screen (File, Home, Insert, Page Layout, Formulas, Data, Review, View, Help, etc.) as tabs. Learn this because I am going to use it about a hundred times throughout this book. Maybe more.

I use the term tab because in the past when one of those options was selected, it looked like the top of a file folder. That's no longer the case. In Excel 2024, the selected tab is just underlined, like here with the Home tab:

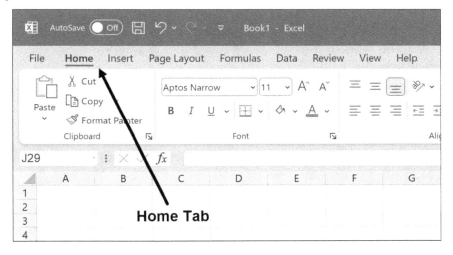

Each tab gives you different tasks you can perform. The Home tab, for example, lets you Paste, Cut, Copy, apply text formatting, and more.

Section

I refer to the different named areas under each tab as a section. The names are at the bottom of the section.

For example, here I have isolated the Font section of the Home tab:

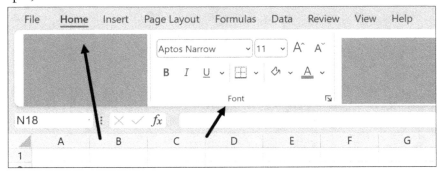

Data

I use the terms data and information interchangeably. Whatever information you have in your worksheet is your data.

Table

I will sometime refer to a table of data or data table. This is just a collection of cells that contain related information and appear to be formatted to belong together.

(In Excel 2024 it looks like Microsoft has introduced a data table concept that is separate and distinct from this. I am not using table or data in that way. We are not that fancy. I just mean a group of data that belong together.)

Scroll Bar

When there is more information than Excel can show you on the screen, it will make scroll bars available so you can "scroll" to see the rest of the information. Scroll bars appear either on the right-hand side or along the bottom when needed.

The primary place you'll see scroll bars is in a worksheet when you have more data in the worksheet than is visible. Here, for example, I have added text into a number of cells in Row 1 and in Column A so that there is data that continues outside of what you can see:

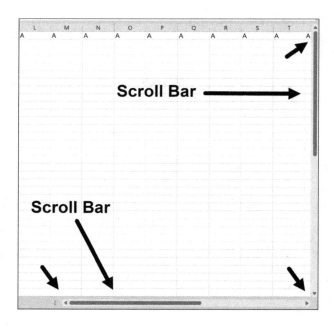

Excel made scroll bars available to navigate all of that data.

Each scroll bar section consists of a light gray scroll area with a darker gray bar that marks where you are in the data. So here, for example, you can see that I am at the very top and far left of the data because the darker gray bars are positioned that way in the scroll bar area.

Scroll bars only let you navigate within the rows and columns where there's data entered. To go past that you can use the arrows at the ends of the scroll bars.

There are a few ways to navigate using scroll bars. One way is to left-click and drag the dark gray bar up and down or side-to-side within the light gray scroll area. As you drag the right-hand bar up or down, or the bottom bar left or right, the visible columns and rows in your worksheet will change.

You can also click into the light gray portion of the scroll bar area to move approximately one screen's worth of columns or rows at a time. It's slower than clicking and dragging the scroll bar itself, but sometimes it's the better option when you want to look through all of the data.

The arrows at the ends will move you one column or row at a time.

Be sure to click into a cell in your current workspace if you use scroll bars to navigate your worksheet. Until you do, if you use Enter or the arrow keys, you'll be moving from whatever cell you were last clicked into, which may be hundreds of rows away. (This happens to me often, especially when using freeze panes, which we'll cover later.)

Select

When I refer to a selected cell it means the cell you're clicked onto, like above with Cell A1 under the definition of cell. As mentioned above, a selected cell will have a different border around it.

It is possible to select a range of cells. To do so with a range of cells that are touching, left-click and drag from a cell at one of the outer corners of the range until all of the cells you want are highlighted.

When you do that, all of the selected cells will be surrounded by a border. Within that border, the first cell you clicked on will be white and the rest will be gray. Like so:

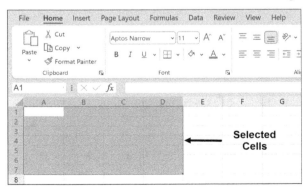

Above I left-clicked on Cell A1 and dragged to Cell D7.

Another way to select cells that are next to each other is to click into the first cell you want, then hold down the Shift key as you use the arrow keys to select other cells.

It is also possible to select cells that aren't touching one another. To do so, select the first cell or range of cells like above, but then hold down the Ctrl key while you select the second cell or range of cells. When selecting ranges of cells, let up on your left-click and drag each time. You can select as many cells or ranges as you want as long as you hold down the Ctrl key each time before you select new cells to add.

(To unselect a cell or cell range, hold down the Ctrl key and click on that cell or cell range again.)

Here I've selected Cells A1 to B2 as well as Cells D3 to E5 and Cells A5 to B5:

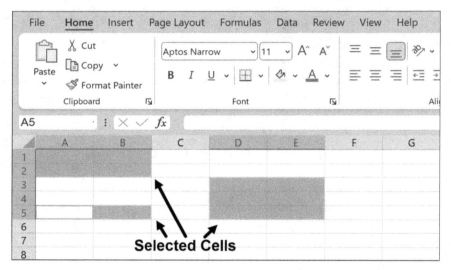

Selected Cells

Each selected range of cells is shaded in gray. The cell I first clicked on for the last selected range, Cell A5, is white with a border around it.

When you have more than one cell selected, the one that's white with a border is the one you can type into, but you can format all selected cells at once. (And what I usually use this for, have Excel take that selected cell range and use it in your formula.)

One final comment. To select an entire column or an entire row, just click on the letter for the column or number for the row around the perimeter of the cells in that worksheet.

Dropdown Menu

I will often refer to dropdown menus or dropdowns, which are a list of potential choices that you can select from that aren't immediately visible. In the set of menu options up top, the existence of a dropdown menu is indicated by an arrow next to that option.

In the image below, you can see dropdown arrows next to Paste, Copy, Font Choice, and Font Size.

I've clicked on the arrow for font choice, and you can now see a dropdown menu of other fonts.

(Note also that there is a scrollbar in the font dropdown menu since there are more available fonts than can be displayed at one time.)

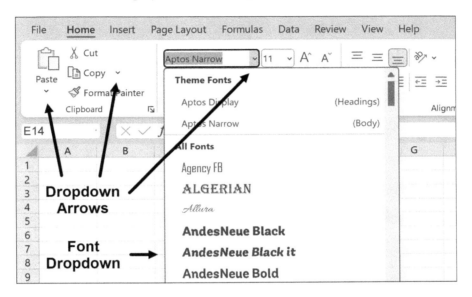

Dialogue Box

Dialogue boxes are pop-up boxes that appear on top of your workspace. They contain a set of available options to choose from. This is the Insert dialogue box, for example:

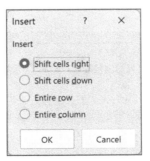

It lets you "insert" cells into a spot on your worksheet. (The number of cells in a worksheet is actually fixed, so what it's really doing is just shifting your existing data to make blank cells available at that particular spot.)

Dialogue boxes are less common now—I think they've largely been replaced by the use of task panes for newer functionality—but they still exist for older functionality, and often contain more options than the menus do.

To close a dialogue box, either make your selection and click OK, click Cancel, or click on the X in the top right corner.

Task Pane

Task panes are separate spaces that can appear to the left, right, or bottom of the worksheet area. They allow you to perform various additional tasks.

The easiest one to see is the Clipboard task pane, which will open if you click on the expansion arrow in the bottom right corner of the Clipboard section of the Home tab:

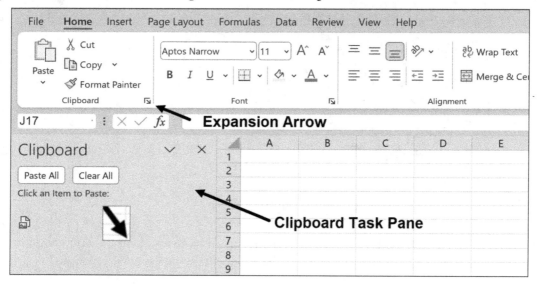

To close a task pane, click on the X in the top right corner of the pane.

Expansion Arrow

Some of the sections in the tabs have what I refer to as expansion arrows. These are arrows in the bottom right corner of that section which open either a dialogue box or a task pane that contains more choices.

For example, the expansion arrow for the Font section of the Home tab will open the Font dialogue box:

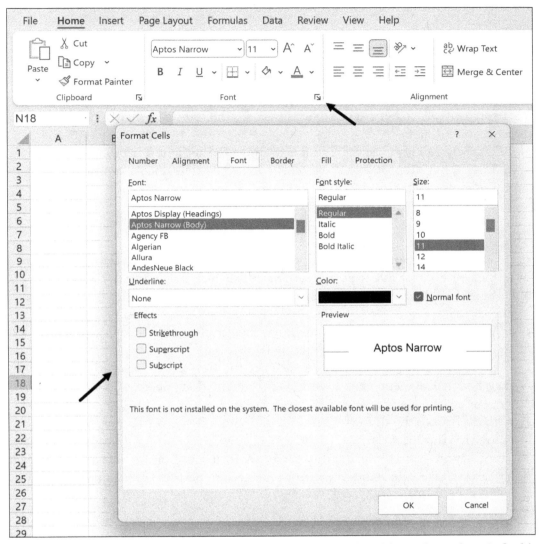

If you are ever looking for something you think you should be able to do and can't find it, it's always worth clicking on one of these to see what else is available.

Cursor

Your cursor is what moves around when you move your mouse. Depending on where you are, it will look like different things. Often in Excel it looks like a variety of arrows, so I may tell you to move the arrow around or the cursor around or even to move the mouse around. All three just mean to get that thing that moves on the screen to a specific spot so you can click.

Pay attention to what your cursor looks like, because the different shapes mean that you can do different things.

Arrow

If I ever tell you to arrow to something, that means to use the arrow keys to navigate to that spot. When you're clicked into a cell in a worksheet, the arrow keys will move you one cell in the direction of the arrow.

(Note that you can also use the Tab key to move to the right one cell, and Shift + Tab to move to the left, but I'll probably avoid telling you to do that since it can be confusing when I refer to the menu options as tabs.)

Control Shortcut

There are various keyboard combinations that you can use in Excel to perform common tasks. I refer to them as control shortcuts, because most use the Ctrl key, but not all of them do. For example, Shift + Tab. A very common one to use is Ctrl + C, which lets you copy your selection.

Note how I write these. I have something, then a plus sign, then something else. That means to hold down both of those keys at the same time.

So to copy, you would hold down the Ctrl key (bottom left of the keyboard for me) and the "c" key. I capitalize them when I write them, but you don't need to do that, just select that letter.

Or, with Shift+Tab, hold down Shift and then press down on Tab as many times as you need to move to your location.

You don't have to learn these, but they can be incredibly useful and time-saving. They mean you don't have to take your hands away from the keys to perform certain tasks, which is very nice.

* * *

Okay, now it's time to dive in on how to actually use Excel.

Absolute Basics

This is the chapter that many may already know and can skip, but it may be worth skimming because you don't know what you don't know. I, for example, never used to use a control shortcut to open a new file until I learned it writing these books. Now I use it regularly.

Open Excel

If you're creating an Excel file from scratch, then your first step needs to be opening Excel, so let's cover that real quick.

If you just installed Microsoft Office, then Excel may be listed in your start menu (generally available by clicking on the Windows icon at the bottom of the screen).

Otherwise, use the search bar at the bottom of your screen or in the start menu to look for Excel. Click on Open when Excel appears on the right-hand side.

I personally like to pin my favorite programs to the bottom of my screen in the taskbar so I can open them easily by just clicking on the icon down there when I need to open Excel.

To do that, you can either right-click on the image of Excel in your search listing and choose Pin to Taskbar (on the left side in the image on the next page).

Or you can expand the menu under Open (on the right side in the image on the next page) and click on it there.

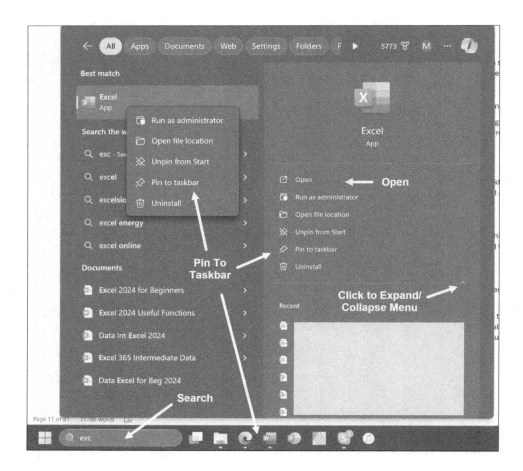

Create a New Excel File

Excel will normally open to the Welcome Screen.

From there the easiest way to start a new Excel file is to click on the Blank Workbook option in the top row.

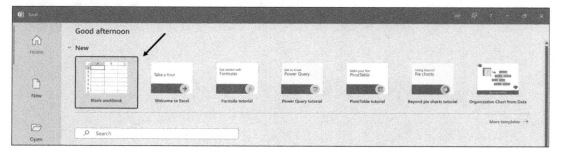

If you're already working in an Excel file and want to open another one, then the easiest choice is to use Ctrl + N.

Or you can click on the File tab to go back to the Welcome Screen where you can then select Blank Workbook.

Open an Existing Excel File

One option for opening an existing Excel file is to go to where you have the file saved and double-click on it. If Excel isn't already open, that will also launch Excel for you.

For files I've worked with before, though, I prefer to open them through Excel. The bottom portion of the Welcome Screen lists the ten Excel files you had open most recently.

Here you can see the top of that section and my three most recent files listed:

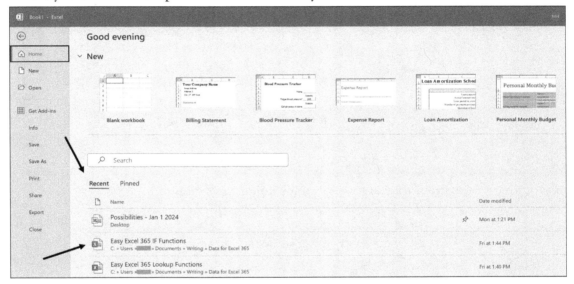

If the file you want is there, just click on the name and it will open.

If it isn't listed but you know you used it sometime recently, click into the white Search field and start typing the file name. When you see the file you want listed as a result, click on the name in the list.

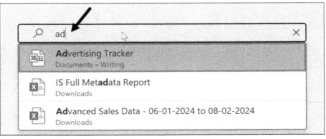

Above, for example, I started to type "ad" because I was looking for my Advertising Tracker file. It gave me three recent files to choose from that have "ad" in the name. I can now click on the first entry in that list, which is the one I was looking for.

A third option you have is to open a file through Excel by navigating to where the file is saved.

To do that, click on the Open option on the left-hand side of the Welcome Screen. That will take you to the Open screen which has Workbooks listed by default but a Folders choice at the top under the Search field. Click on that. It will then show you a list of folders that contain Excel files you recently used:

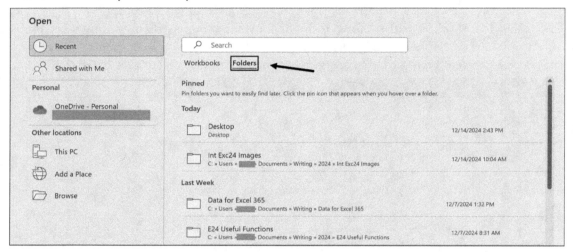

Click on one of the listed folders to see any sub-folders or Excel files.

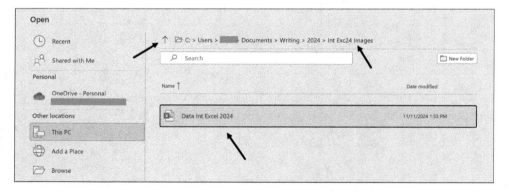

Once you find the file you want, click on it to open it. If you don't find the file you want, you can use the up arrow next to the file path at the top to go back one level and see other folders.

If that still doesn't get you there, then click on Browse, which will bring up the Open dialogue box.

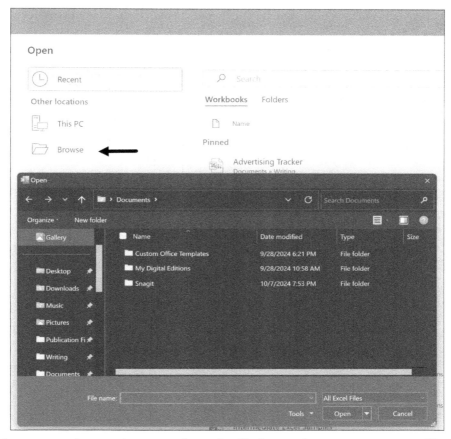

At that point you can just navigate to where the file is saved on your computer like you would have outside of Excel. When you find the file, double-click on it, or click on the name and then click on Open at the bottom corner of the dialogue box.

Pin A File

I have certain files that I go back to over and over. One is that possibilities file you see in the screenshots above, which is actually my budgeting workbook (that is discussed in detail in *Excel for Budgeting*).

I want to be able to find that immediately no matter how many Excel files I've opened in the meantime. The way to make that happen is to pin the file. That makes the file always available in a special list you can access from the Welcome Screen.

To pin a file, hold your mouse to the left of the date modified, like I'm doing here for Easy Excel 365 Lookup Functions:

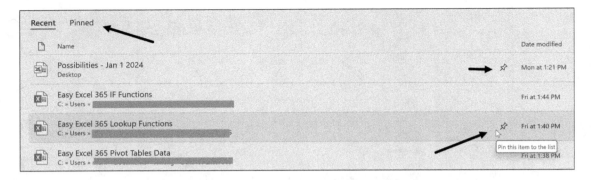

You can see that a text box appeared that says "Pin this item to the list" along with a thumbtack image. Left-click and the file will be pinned. That thumbtack image will remain for that file.

To see your pinned files at any time, click on Pinned at the top of the file listing, and it will switch over to a list that is only your pinned files. Like so:

To unpin a file, just left-click on the pin for that file.

Close a File

The easiest way to close a file is to click on the X in the top right corner when you have the file open:

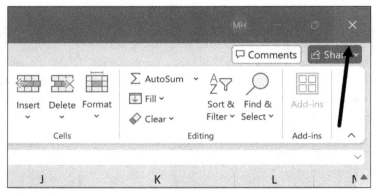

(And, really in Excel, almost anything you can close will have an X in that top right corner, so learn that one well.)

If that was the only Excel file you had open, it will also close Excel.

Another option is to use the control shortcut, Ctrl + W. Or you can go to the File tab and choose Close on the left-hand side menu. Both of those options will keep Excel open.

Save a File

Excel works pretty hard to make sure you don't close a file without saving your changes, so any file that has a change in it that you try to close will pop up with a dialogue box asking if you want to save those changes:

That's probably one of the easiest ways to save changes to a file that you're done with. Just hit Enter when that dialogue box appears and your changes will be saved.

Another option, for a file you're not ready to close, is to use the save icon in the top left corner:

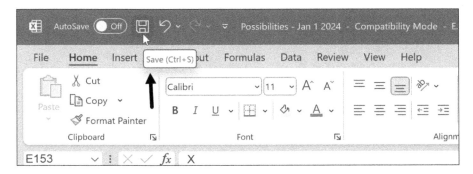

You can also use the control shortcut, Ctrl + S.

All three of the above work great for an existing file where you want to keep the file name, file location, and file type the same, which will be most of the time.

But for a new file there are more steps. When you choose to Save using one of the above methods, Excel will present you with a Save dialogue box where it will ask you for a file name, location, and type. It suggests default values for you:

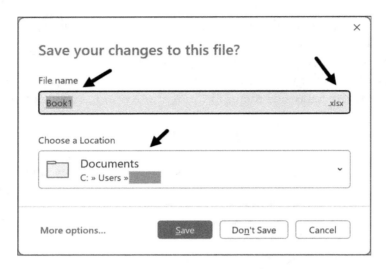

But it is very likely you will want a name other than Book1. That name will already be selected so you just need to type to change the name.

The dropdown for location will show other recent file locations. To choose a location not available in the dropdown, or to change the file type, click on More Options. That will open the Save As dialogue box.

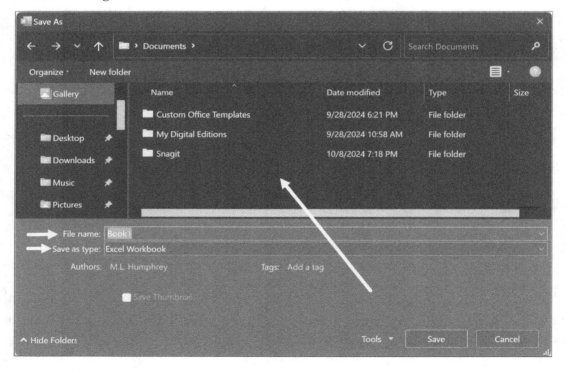

Save As For an Existing File

There are going to be times where you have an existing file but you want to either give it a new name, save it to a new location, or change the file type. When that happens, go to the File tab and choose Save As from the left-hand menu. (See next page.)

Click on one of the listed folder names or click on Browse to bring up the Save As dialogue box.

The File Name field is where you can change the file name.

The Save As Type is a dropdown menu where you can choose a different file type. The standard now is Excel Workbook which is also an .xlsx file. That will usually be fine. But you may run into somebody who needs an older file format. In that case, use Excel 97-2003 Workbook which is also an .xls file. (You may also inherit an older file that's in .xls format and need to upgrade it so you can have the full benefit of Excel 2024.)

The other file type you may run into is a .csv file type. A lot of data output is provided in that format. Excel is going to open it just fine most of the time, but it's a good idea to save it as an .xlsx, Excel Workbook, format if you do any sort of calculations or manipulations with the data.

To choose a new file location, navigate to that location using the side menu and/or folders, just like you would to find a file.

Rename a File

If all you want to do is change a file name and you don't need to keep two versions of the file, then don't use Save As. Instead, go to where the file is saved, click on the file name once to select the file, and then click on it again to highlight the name and make it editable.

Type in the new name you want, click away, and you're done.

Keep in mind that a renamed file cannot then be opened from the recent files list in Excel. Excel will still be looking for that old file name, so won't be able to find the file under its new name. If that's important, your best bet is to rename the file and then immediately open it so the new name is listed in your recent files list.

Move a File

You also should not use Save As if all you really wanted to do was move a file. That also should be done outside of Excel.

Go to where the file is currently saved. Click on it to select it, use Ctrl +X to cut, go to the new location, and use Ctrl + V to paste.

If you're not comfortable using control shortcuts, you can also select the file and then choose the pair of scissors in the top row of the dialogue box or right-click and choose the scissors from the dropdown menu to cut.

You can then go to the folder where you want to place the file and click on the image for paste which looks like a stylized version of a clipboard with a piece of paper on it. You can also right-click and choose the icon from the dropdown menu that appears.

Delete a File

If you ever want to permanently delete a file, that also needs to be done outside of Excel. Go to where the file is located. Click on it and then click on the image of a trashcan in the top of the dialogue box. You can also right-click on the file and choose the trash can from there.

Be careful that you only have the file you want to delete selected and not anything else. (As I have learned from personal experience.)

If you do accidentally delete something you didn't want to, and notice it immediately, use Ctrl + Z to Undo.

Keep in mind that for most computers, a deleted file will be sent to the Recycle Bin and may remain there, capable of being restored, until you proactively go and empty that recycle bin. Excel won't be able to open it though, and you'll get an error message if you try to do so from the files list in Excel.

Navigating Excel

Now it's time to talk about how you move around within Excel. We'll talk about how to actually enter values in the next chapter.

Basic Navigation Within a Worksheet

When you open a new Blank Workbook, Excel you will automatically start in Cell A1 of Sheet 1. For an existing file, you're going to start where you left off. So whatever worksheet and cell where you last were.

The easiest way to move to a different cell in a worksheet is to left-click on it.

The arrow keys will also move you one cell in the direction of the arrow. So use the right arrow to go right, the up arrow to go up, etc.

The Tab key will move you one cell to the right. Shift + Tab will move you one cell to the left.

Enter will move you down. If there's no data in your worksheet, you'll go down to the next row in that same column. If you have data that is organized and you've been consistently completing that data across multiple columns row after row, then Enter might take you to the first empty column in that range in the next row.

Here, for example, I have created a simple data table with three columns of data to enter. When I input the first set of values in Cells A2 through C2 and then hit Enter, it took me to *Cell A3* not cell C3. After I entered information in Cells A3 through C3 and hit Enter it took me to Cell A4.

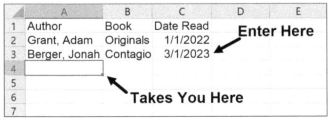

The PgUp and PgDn keys will also work to move you up or down one visible set of rows at a time.

If the cell, row, or column you want isn't visible, then use the scroll bars to get there. Clicking and dragging the dark gray bar is the fastest way to move when there is existing data, but if you don't have data in those rows or columns yet you'll need to use the arrows at the ends of the scroll bars.

Another option is to use the scroll wheel on your mouse.

Just remember with scrolling to click into an actual cell when you get to where you want to go, because otherwise when you type, hit Enter, use the arrow keys, etc. you will still be doing so from that last cell you were clicked into.

Insert a New Worksheet

To add another worksheet to your workbook, the easiest option is to click on the plus sign next to the name of your existing worksheet(s):

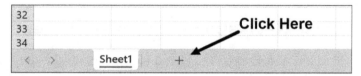

This will insert a worksheet to the right of the one you're currently on.

You can also right-click on an existing worksheet's name , and choose Insert from the dropdown menu. Click on Worksheet (it should be selected by default) and then OK when the Insert dialogue box appears. This will insert a worksheet to the left of the one you right-clicked on.

Another option is to go to the Cells section of the Home tab, click on the dropdown arrow under Insert, and choose Insert Sheet from there.

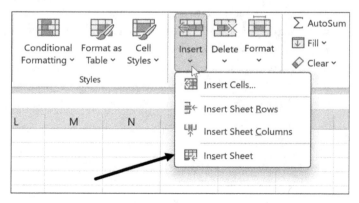

This will also insert a worksheet to the left of the sheet you are currently on.

Select a Worksheet

To select the worksheet you want to see, click on the name tab at the bottom of the workspace:

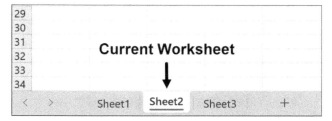

A selected worksheet will be white instead of gray and the name will also be underlined. See here that I have Sheet2 selected and Sheet1 and Sheet3 are more in the background.

(It is possible to select more than one worksheet at a time. I do not recommend it for a beginner. If that ever accidentally happens, click on a different worksheet to unselect all currently selected worksheets. You can also right-click on one of the sheets and choose Ungroup Sheets from the dropdown menu.)

Move a Worksheet

To move a worksheet, simply left-click on the worksheet name and drag to where you want it to go. As you drag along the row of worksheets, you'll see a little arrow that indicates where the sheet will move. Just let up on your left-click and it will drop into that new location.

Rename a Worksheet

Once you have more than one worksheet, chances are you'll want to name them something other than Sheet1, Sheet 2, etc. To rename a worksheet, you can either double-click on the worksheet name, or right-click on it and choose Rename from the dropdown menu:

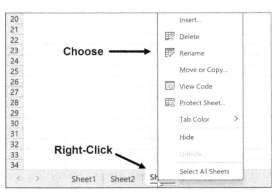

Either option will highlight the name of the worksheet. From there just type in what you want the name to be and hit Enter or click away. You can use Esc to cancel if you decide you don't want to change the name after all.

There are restrictions on how long the worksheet name can be (31 characters) and what characters you can use. Excel 2024 won't let you type past that point, nor will it let you use one of the restricted characters, so if you were typing just fine and now can't type something it's probably safe to assume that's the reason.

Delete a Worksheet

To delete a worksheet, right-click on the worksheet name and choose Delete from the dropdown menu. You can also select the worksheet and then go to the Delete dropdown menu in the Cells section of the Home tab and choose Delete Sheet.

Excel will delete a blank worksheet immediately.

If there is any data in the worksheet, Excel will show a dialogue box asking you to confirm the deletion. Click on Delete to proceed or click on Cancel if you want to double-check what's in there first.

Basic Navigation Between Worksheets

If you have more worksheets than you can see at the bottom of the workspace, use the arrows on the bottom left corner to move the set of visible worksheets left or right by one sheet at time.

Use Ctrl while clicking on the left or right arrows to move all the way to either end of your listed worksheets.

Copy a Worksheet

To keep one version of a worksheet where it already is and create a copy of a worksheet and move it somewhere else, right-click on the worksheet name, and choose the Move or Copy option from the dropdown menu.

This will open the Move or Copy dialogue box, which you can see on the opposie page.

Check the box towards the bottom that says Create a Copy.

You then need to tell Excel where to put the worksheet. If it's in the current workbook, then click on the worksheet name that is one past where you want to place your copied worksheet. Click OK.

If you want to place it in another workbook, use the dropdown menu at the top where it says To Book and select that workbook name.

You can also just move it to a new workbook by selecting (new book) in the dropdown.

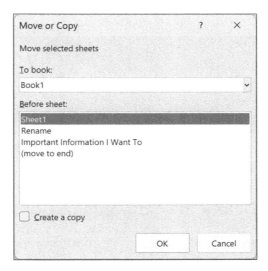

To be listed in that dropdown, a workbook needs to already be open. If it isn't, use Esc or Cancel, go and open that workbook, and then try again.

Move a Worksheet to a Different Workbook

The process to move a worksheet to a different workbook is the exact same as copying it to one, you just don't check the box for Create a Copy.

Select a Column or Row

We already covered this in the terminology section, but I want to cover it again. To select an entire column or row, just click on the letter for that column or the number for that row. Here, for example, I have clicked on the letter "D" to select Column D:

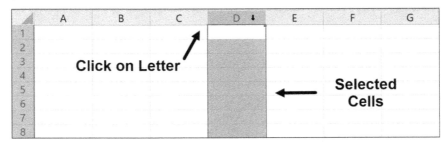

You can see that the cells in that column are all now shaded and also the name of the column is colored differently.

To select more than one column or row at a time, left-click and drag across the letters or numbers for those columns or rows. You can also click on the first column or row in the range, hold down the Shift key, and click on the last one. If they are not all touching, hold down the Ctrl key as you select each one.

Delete a Column or Row

To delete a column, row, or range of columns or rows, select them first and then right-click and choose Delete from the dropdown menu.

You can also select them and then go to the Cells section of the Home tab and use the Delete dropdown. Choose Delete Sheet Rows or Delete Sheet Columns, as appropriate.

Delete the Contents of Cells

Delete will delete the content in all of a range of selected cells.

Backspace will just delete the content in the first cell of the last cell range you clicked on.

Another option is to go to the Editing section of the Home tab and use the Clear dropdown. Clear Contents will clear the text, formulas, etc. but leave the formatting. Clear All will delete the contents as well as any formatting.

Delete a Cell in a Worksheet

Deleting columns or rows is relatively straightforward, because everything else in the worksheet stays properly aligned. Everything that was in Column C may move to Column B, but it's still all in one column.

Deleting cells can be trickier because you're taking part of a row or column and removing it. The other cells in the worksheet have to shift to fill that space. Since you're usually not going to do this if you don't have data in that worksheet, you need to pay attention to the rest of the data in the worksheet.

If you only delete part of a row or column, then data that has to move to fill the deleted space can get out of alignment.

It is relatively easy in Excel to "break" your data. Let's look at that little table I was building before:

	A	B	C	D
1	Author	Book	Date Read	
2	Grant, Adam	Originals	1/1/2022	
3	Berger, Jonah	Contagious	3/1/2023	
4	Godin, Seth	Linchpin	4/1/2021	
5	Clear, James	Atomic Habits	7/6/2022	
6				

This is a pretty basic table of data where I'm listing the author, title, and date read for some books on my shelf. You and I can look at that and know that everything on Row 3 belongs together.

According to this made-up data, I read Contagious by Jonah Berger on 3/1/23, right?

Now, here's where the problem happens. If I delete Cell C3, Excel has to shift things somehow to fill in that gap. I can choose to shift cells left or to shift cells up. If I make the wrong choice and choose to shift up, I get this:

	A	B	C	D	E
1	Author	Book	Date Read		
2	Grant, Adam	Originals	1/1/2022		
3	Berger, Jonah	Contagious	4/1/2021		
4	Godin, Seth	Linchpin	7/6/2022		
5	Clear, James	Atomic Habits			
6					

See how the data broke? It now looks like I read that book on 4/1/21 instead, and that I read Linchpin on 7/6/22 instead of 4/1/21. I broke my data. In a normal data table that you create by inputting information in Excel, that can happen very easily.

So when you delete cells in a worksheet, pay attention to what effect that will have on *all* of the data in the worksheet, not just the cells around what you delete.

This is why sometimes it is best to delete an entire row or column to keep things like that from happening. It may also mean deleting more cells to keep everything together. If I'm deleting Cell C3, I really should delete Cells A3 and B3, too. (Or I could just remove the text in Cell C3, but not delete the cell.)

Okay. Lecture over, let's walk through how you actually delete a cell.

Select the cell or cells you want to delete, and then right-click and choose Delete from the dropdown menu.

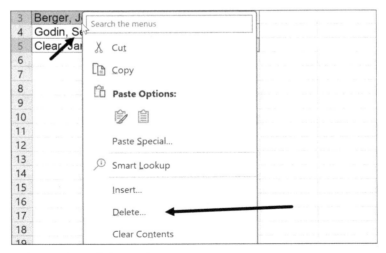

That will bring up the Delete dialogue box:

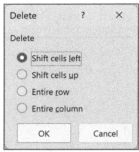

You have two choices there, shift cells up or shift cells left. How do you want to fill in that empty space? When your cell or cells are removed, do you want everything below that to move up, or do you want everything to the right to move over? The appropriate choice is going to depend on your remaining data.

In our example above, I should've chosen to shift cells left. The rest of the table would've remained untouched if I'd done so.

Note that you can also choose to delete an entire row or column using that dialogue box. It's another way to do that without having to select the entire row or column.

Another option is to select your cell(s) you want to delete and then use the Delete dropdown in the Cells section of the Home tab, which will also bring up the Delete dialogue box.

Insert a Column, Row, or Cell

Insert basically works like delete except the Insert dialogue box gives the option of shifting the cells right or down to make room for your inserted cells. Again, this only makes sense to do if you're dealing with cells that already have information in them because the size of an Excel worksheet is fixed.

You can either right-click on selected cells, and choose Insert, or you can use the Insert dropdown in the Cells section of the Home tab.

As with deleting cells, pay attention to your other data to make sure that you aren't breaking your data relationships when you insert cells.

Find Text

I cover advanced find in *Intermediate Excel 2024*, but real quick, if you need to find text in a formula or cell in an Excel worksheet, you can use Ctrl + F to open the Find and Replace dialogue box. Type the text you need to find into the white space next to Find What and then click on Find Next. Excel will take you to the next cell that has that text in it.

Find All will give you a list of all of the locations in your worksheet that have that text in a cell. You can then click on the entries in the list to move to each one.

By default, Find works within one worksheet at a time not the entire workbook. It also is not case-sensitive and looks for the text you tell it to look for in any part of a cell. It does not look at the results of any formulas.

One thing to be aware of in Excel is that it will search in columns or rows that are hidden, too. So sometimes you may think that Excel hasn't moved to the next cell with that value in it, but it really has, it's just not a cell that's visible to you.

Input and Delete Data

At its most basic, inputting data into Excel is very easy. You click into a cell and start typing. When you're done, you hit Enter. Or tab. Or arrow or click to another cell.

But there's a lot more that can go into it, which is what this chapter covers.

Undo

My lifesaver when working in Excel is the ability to undo things. I use Ctrl + Z, which is the control shortcut to undo, all the time. You can use it multiple times in a row if you mess up and don't realize it for a few steps.

It does go back through each thing you did in order, so if you messed up ten steps ago, you'll lose all ten things you've done since then. But better than not being able to, right?

If you know up front that you have a lot of steps to reverse, you can use the Undo dropdown menu available in the top left corner of Excel.

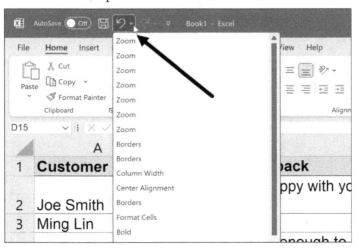

Click on the backwards pointing arrow once to undo your last step, or click on the dropdown arrow next to it and Excel will show you the last 100 things that you did in Excel.

In the image on the previous page, you can see that the last few things I did was zoomed in, added some borders to cells, changed a column width, and more. So if I want to undo that Bold of some text, I'd also lose all of that.

I can do it, though. I just need to click on Bold and that step and everything that came after it will be undone.

Undo is fabulous to use throughout Excel, not just when inputting data. It's one of the easiest ways to undo mistakes when you're learning.

But there are a few places it doesn't work well. For example, if you input the text, "October 4", Excel will treat that like a date and a simple Undo will not change that cell back to text.

99 times out of 100, though, Undo is the way to back out of a mistake in Excel.

Redo

What if you Undo, like I just did, and then realize that was a mistake and want to Redo?

You can either use Ctrl + Y to redo one step at a time, or you can use the Redo arrow up top, which will only be available to select if you already undid something.

It's the arrow that points to the right and it also has a dropdown menu.

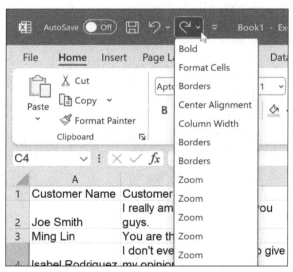

Click on a step in that list and it will redo each step in the list above the one you chose as well as that one.

(Excel will highlight the entries in gray that it's going to redo as you move your cursor over the list to make your selection.)

Same thing with Redo as with Undo, it does them all in order, you can't pick and choose.

Esc

Another little trick I like to use often is Esc. If I start typing a formula in a cell and it becomes a hot mess, I just use the Esc key to get away from whatever I was typing and start over.

It's also a good way to back out of something you've started. Say you copy some data and were going to paste it elsewhere but then change your mind, use Esc to be done with that.

It will also turn off a tool like Format Painter.

Between Undo and Esc that should get you out of 95% of the scrapes you get into. Think of Undo as "Didn't mean to do that, sorry, can we go back?" and Esc as "Wait, let me just stop what I'm doing right now."

Also, if you're ever inputting data and try to Undo and it doesn't work, you may need to use Esc first to back out and then Undo from there.

Okay. On to the inputting text tricks.

Display The Contents of a Cell as Text

If you start the text you enter into a cell with a minus sign (-), plus sign (+), or equals sign (=), Excel will think you're about to enter a formula in that cell. Excel also tries very, very hard to recognize text ("October 2024") as dates and convert them for you, often when you don't want it to.

Fortunately, there is a very simple workaround for these issues. Simply type a single quote mark at the start of the text you're entering into that cell.

So if you want to have an entry that looks like this:

-Item A

what you need to actually type is:

'-Item A

Or if you want:

October 2024

What you need to type is:

'October 2024

Simple as that. The single quote mark is not visible in the worksheet and it won't be visible when you print either. It's just a way to tell Excel "Leave this as is, please".

Include Line Breaks In a Cell

Most people think of using Excel for numbers, but I actually use it for text a lot.

For example, my current day job requires a lot of analysis of bank statements. Sure, bank statements include the dollar value, but just as important in that data is the name of the person who received or sent the money.

Also, I've used Excel in the past for a complex analysis of credit agency regulations across various jurisdictions, because Excel has the ability to filter entries.

Sometimes I want my text to appear on separate lines within one single cell. But you can't just use Enter to make that happen, because Enter will take you to a new cell.

The trick is to use Alt + Enter. If you hold down the Alt key and use the Enter key, Excel will create a line break *within* the cell. Like so:

	A	B	C
1	Rule Number	Text of Rule without Line Breaks	Text of Rule with Line Breaks
2	11-51-501	(1) It is unlawful for any person, in connection with the offer, sale, or purchase of any security, directly or indirectly: (a) To employ any device, scheme, or artifice to defraud; (b) To make any untrue statement of a material fact or to omit to state a material fact necessary in order to make the statements made, in the light of the circumstances under which they are made, not misleading; or (c) To engage in any act, practice, or course of business which operates or would operate as a fraud or deceit upon any person.	(1) It is unlawful for any person, in connection with the offer, sale, or purchase of any security, directly or indirectly: (a) To employ any device, scheme, or artifice to defraud; (b) To make any untrue statement of a material fact or to omit to state a material fact necessary in order to make the statements made, in the light of the circumstances under which they are made, not misleading; or (c) To engage in any act, practice, or course of business which operates or would operate as a fraud or deceit upon any person.

In the image above I used Alt + Enter twice for each break, once to move the text to the next line and once to create that blank line between the sections. See how it makes things much easier to read? Very handy to know.

Auto-Suggested Text

Within a column of data, Excel will by default try to help you by suggesting text that matches what you've entered before. Often when I'm entering data and have control over what I enter, I use this feature to speed things up. It only works with letters or combinations of letters and numbers (it doesn't work with just numbers), so I may sometimes write something as ABC123 rather than 123ABC to save input time if I have that kind of control over my data.

What it does is looks at what you're entering and compares it to your previous entries. If what you have entered so far is a unique match for an entry above, Excel will suggest that entry for you. Let me show you:

On the next page is the table I created earlier for formatting data. I clicked into Cell A5 and typed the letter "j". Excel automatically looked at the other values in Column A and suggested that the entry I want is "Joe Smith" since I only have one entry in that column that starts with a J.

	A	B	C
1	**Customer Name**	**Customer Feedback**	**Customer Score**
2	Joe Smith	I really am not happy with you guys.	1
3	Ming Lin	You are the best.	5
4	Isabel Rodriguez	I don't even care enough to give my opinion.	3
5	joe Smith		
6			

Suggested Text

If I agree, I can hit Enter or tab or arrow away from the cell and Excel will populate Cell A5 with "Joe Smith". I only had to type one character instead of nine. Great, right?

If you have a value like 123ABC, though, Excel will not try to suggest anything until you type the "A" even if the only 123 entry is 123ABC.

Also, Excel only does this if there's a unique value it can suggest. So if you have "Joe Smith" in one field and "Joe P. Smith" in another, it won't suggest anything until you get to "Joe P" or "Joe S", because until that point there isn't a unique value to suggest.

Another nice thing about auto-suggested text is it carries over the formatting from the suggested entry. So I can write "Joe Smith" all nicely capitalized, but the next time around I just have to type "j" and not worry about capitalization.

If Excel suggests a value that you don't want to use, then just keep typing.

F2

This is probably a good time to mention F2. If you click on a cell and use F2, it will take you to the end of whatever text you have entered into that cell. This comes in very useful if you just need to make one small change at the end of a cell. So, say I have an entry for "Maria Castilla Ladaron" and I type M and the auto-suggested text gives me that full name, but I want to add "Hernandez" on the end. I can leave that cell and let Excel populate it with the "Maria Castilla Ladaron", and then go back to the cell, use F2 to get right to the end of the text, and type in Hernandez. And done.

I also will use this is if I have entries like Author A, Author B, Author C, and Excel isn't recognizing that as a pattern for Auto Fill. I'll copy Author A to all of my cells and then go back to the ones that should be Author B, Author C, etc. and use F2, to change that A at the end.

Auto Fill

Excel has the ability to recognize patterns and fill those in for you. Some patterns, it only takes one entry. Other patterns, it never figures out.

Here is an example:

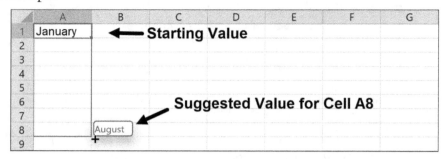

In Cell A1 I entered the value "January". I then left-clicked on the bottom right corner of that cell and dragged downward. As I dragged downward to Cells A2, A3, etc. Excel briefly showed me what value it thought I would want in each of those cells.

Here you can see that I'm at Cell A8 and it's suggesting August after having suggested February, March, April, etc. Perfect.

If I then let up on my left-click, Excel will populate Cells A2 through A8 with the suggested values. Like so:

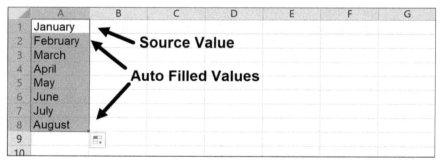

I only had to enter January and then click and drag and Excel did all the rest of the work for me.

I could have clicked and dragged to the right just as easily as I dragged downward. It would have populated values across Row 1 instead of down Column A.

Obviously, not all patterns can be recognized with one value. If you have a custom pattern, you may need a few entries before Excel can identify it. On the next page I have three entries, "Book 1", "Book 2", and "Book 3". I highlighted all three, clicked in the bottom right corner of Cell A3, and dragged, and Excel caught the pattern. You can see it will put "Book 9" in Cell A9.

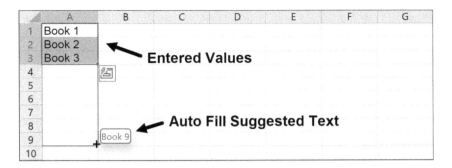

Copy Values Down a Column

If you have a large data table, you can have Excel fill that entire column quickly by double left-clicking in the bottom right corner. As long as there is a column next to the one you're trying to populate that tells Excel how far to go, it will auto-fill all the way down for you.

I actually use this to copy values quickly. Excel will auto fill with a series of values. I then go to the bottom of the portion of the list that is visible on my screen and find what I'm going to call the Auto Fill Options widget:

There is a dropdown arrow next to that image. Click on it and you will see a list of options:

To change the auto fill over to a copy of that starting value, just click on the circle next to Copy Cells. And done.

How to Customize Your Excel Input Options

My current employer uses Office 365, and I have noticed recently that Excel is getting a little too proactive in trying to auto fill values for me. As in, it's doing it on its own without telling me, and not waiting for me to affirmatively tell it to do so. If you run into that issue, you can turn this off.

To do so, go to the File tab, click on Options in the bottom left corner, and when the Excel Options dialogue box appears, go to the Advanced tab:

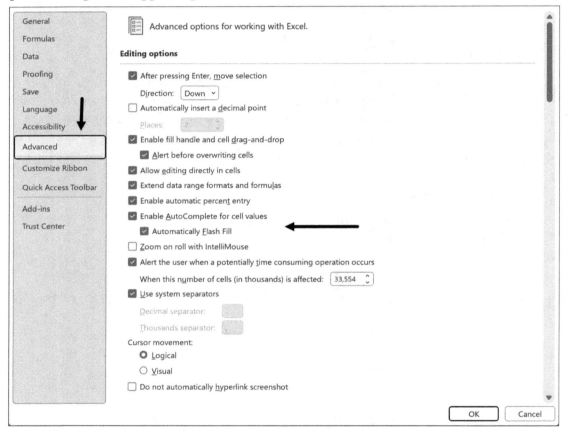

Uncheck the box for "Automatically Flash Fill".

If you like that Excel suggests a word for you like above with our "Jim Smith" then leave the Enable Autocomplete box checked.

While we're here. Go to the Data tab and you'll see a section called Automatic Data Conversion:

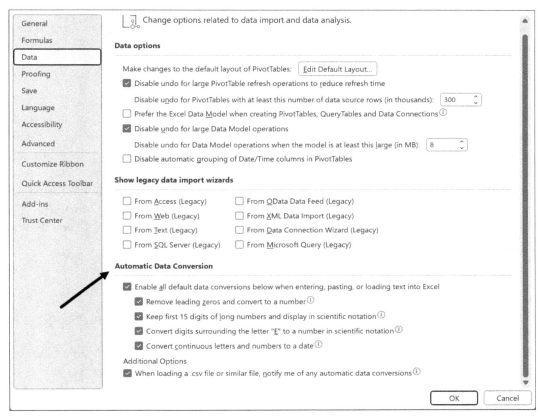

You may want to uncheck one or more of these boxes. For example, I work with zip codes a lot. Some of those have a zero at the start. I can either use the single quote mark (') to tell Excel to leave them alone, format the cell as a zip code, or I can uncheck the box for "remove leading zeros" and Excel will stop turning a zip code that is 01234 into 1234 on me. (Theoretically.)

Note that if you do that, the value stores as text not a number, which for zip codes is fine with me.

I also deal with ISBN numbers which are fifteen digits long and which Excel loves to put into scientific notation. "12345678912345" becomes "1.23457E+13", so I can uncheck that next box, too, although I just did so and it didn't work.

Oddly enough, when I clicked into the cell where I had the value, copied the value, and pasted it into another cell formatted as a text cell, where it still didn't work, somehow the original cell started displaying properly. And then the second one did, too. (Excel is not always perfect. And sometimes they break things while working on other things. It's a very old program with lots of layers of functionality that have been added or refined over the years, and occasionally there will be quirks. Sometimes it really is them not you. Although often enough it will be you. Or me as the case may be.)

So those last two fixes may or may not help, but the Flash Fill one is a lifesaver. Turn that nonsense off.

Delete Text From a Cell

We already discussed how to use Delete to delete the contents of a cell and Clear to delete formatting as well. But if you don't want to delete everything in a cell, but instead just edit part of the contents, then either double-click on that cell to be able to move to a specific spot in that text, or left-click on the cell and then use the formula bar.

From wherever you are in that text in that cell Delete will remove one character (space, letter, number, etc.) to the right and Backspace will remove one character to the left.

You can also select multiple characters in a cell and then use Backspace or Delete to remove your selection.

Add More Text To a Cell

You can add more text to a cell by double-clicking on it or left-clicking on it and going to the formula bar and typing what you need in the spot where it's needed.

By default, the formula bar will only show one line of text. I usually double-click on the cell itself in those situations, but there is an arrow at the end of the formula bar that will expand that to three lines and provide up and down arrows for you to use to see the rest of the text.

Freeze Panes

One final trick for you with respect to inputting data is to know how to use Freeze Panes. Most tables of data you create are going to have a header row that tells you what is in each column. Some may also have a column or two on the left-hand side that tells you what the row of data covers, like a student or customer name.

But as you enter more data in Excel, those rows or columns will disappear. When you get to Row 652 of your data, Row 1 isn't going to be visible anymore. Fortunately, you can use Freeze Panes, which is available in the Window section of the View tab, to tell Excel to keep certain rows or columns always visible.

The dropdown menu for Freeze Panes will give you the choice to Freeze Panes, Freeze Top Row, or Freeze First Column.

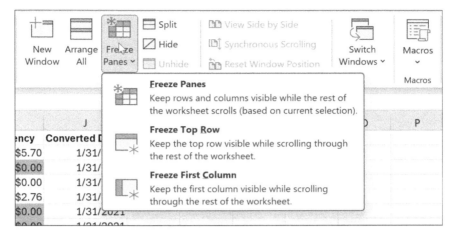

Freeze Top Row will freeze the top row in your visible workspace. So if you want to always be able to see Row 1, be sure it's showing on your workspace before you choose this option.

If you have a data table that starts on Row 10, you can scroll in your workspace until Row 10 is the top row visible, and then choose this option. That will make Rows 1 through 9 permanently hidden until you turn it off, but you will have Row 10 visible at the top of the worksheet even when you're on Row 710.

Same concept works for Freeze First Column. It will keep the first column that was visible in the workspace when you turned it on visible as you scroll to the right. Any columns to the left of that will be hidden until you turn Freeze Panes off.

The final option, Freeze Panes, lets you freeze both columns and rows at the same time as well as more than one row or column at a time. To use this one, arrange your workspace so that the columns and rows you need to be able to see at all times are visible, and then click into the first cell that you *don't* want to have to see (so the one to the right and below the rows and columns you want frozen), and then choose Freeze Panes.

After you turn on freeze panes, you may want to scroll in each direction to make sure that what you're seeing is what you intended to be able to see/not see.

To turn off freeze panes, just go back to that dropdown. You'll see an Unfreeze Panes option. Click on it.

Copy, Cut, and Paste Data

There are going to be times when you need to take information that's in one location in an Excel workbook and move it or use it elsewhere. So copying, moving (known as cutting in Excel), and pasting data is an essential Excel skill to master.

First step, is to select your data. We touched on it before, but let's cover it in more detail now.

Select Cell(s)

To select the information in one cell, just click on the cell.

To select information in cells that are next to each other, left-click on the first or last cell in the cell range and then drag until all of the cells you want are selected.

You can drag in any direction, but that starting cell needs to be in the corner of the range. If you click on one cell, drag right, and then reverse direction and drag left past the first cell, the only cells selected will be from the first cell to the left.

Another way to select a range of cells is to click on the first or last cell in the range, hold down the Shift key, and then click on the cell at the other end of the range.

If you have a data table where the top row and first column of cells are continuously populated with data, then you can click into the top left corner of the table and use Shift + Ctrl + down arrow + right arrow to quickly select all of the cells in the table.

This is very useful when you have large data tables. It's much faster to use Shift + Ctrl to select the data than to try to highlight the rows by clicking and dragging, even though that is doable. (And what I used to do back in the day.)

Just be careful if there are any breaks in your rows or columns because Excel will stop at a blank cell when you use Shift + Ctrl and the arrow keys.

If you need to select cells that aren't touching, then use the Ctrl key to do that. You can combine Ctrl with selecting ranges. So you could select a range of cells, hold down the Ctrl key, and select another range of cells.

To select an entire Column, click on the letter for the column.

To select an entire Row, click on the number for the row.

To select more than one column or row, treat them like cells. Select the first one, and then left-click and drag or use the Ctrl or Shift keys.

Select All

There are going to be times when you want to select all of the data on a worksheet. I will often do this with a worksheet that has formulas so that I can copy the data and replace it with just the results of those formulas. This lets me lock in my results and is often useful when I'm using Excel formulas to transform my data in some way.

To easily select all of the cells on a worksheet, you have two options. One, click anywhere in the worksheet and then use Ctrl + A. Two, you can click in the top left corner of the worksheet where the rows and columns intersect:

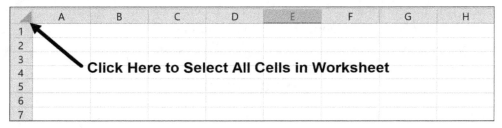

After you Select All, that darker gray triangle will turn green and all of your cells will show that they've been selected.

Terminology

To leave the original data where it is but take an exact duplicate of that data to put elsewhere, you Copy. Easy enough.

To move that data from where it is and put it elsewhere, you Cut.

To place the data in its new location, whether you were copying or cutting, you Paste.

Copy and Paste Data As Is

By default, your data that you copy or cut is going to keep its formatting in its new location. This is the "as is" part. So if it was bolded and bright red, it will stay that way in its new location. If it was highlighted yellow and had a border, same. It all moves.

As defined above, copying data means you leave the original where it is and take an exact duplicate of that data to move elsewhere.

First step, select the cells that contain what you want to copy.

Second step, copy. I generally copy by using Ctrl + C. It's one of the control shortcuts I really recommend you learn because it will save you a ton of time in using Excel.

But if you forget the control shortcut, there are a couple other options. You can go to the Clipboard section of the Home tab and click on the Copy option there:

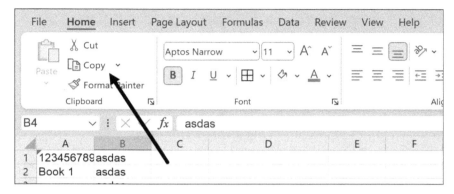

(You don't need the dropdown, just click on the two pieces of paper image.)

Or you can right-click on your selected cells and choose Copy from the dropdown menu:

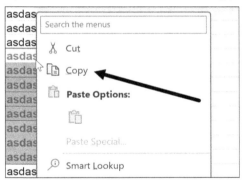

All three get you the same result. Your selected cells will now have a moving dashed border around them, and Excel will be ready for you to paste a copy of those cell contents into a new location.

For the third step, click on the first cell where you want to copy the information to. That can be in the current worksheet, another worksheet, another workbook, or even somewhere like a Word document.

Fourth step, paste. Once again, I tend to use the control shortcut for this, Ctrl + V. But if you only need to paste the data once, you can also just hit Enter.

There are other paste options. For example, you can go to the Clipboard section of the Home tab and click on the Paste option there, or you can right-click and choose the first Paste option from the dropdown menu.

You can see both of those here:

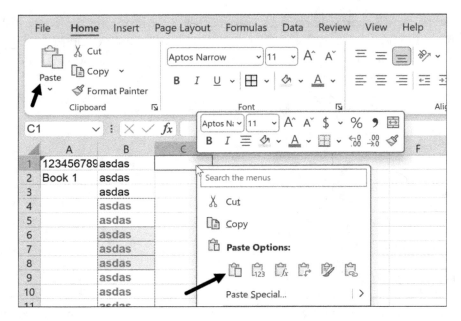

Once you are done pasting your data, if you didn't do it using Enter, then use Esc or click into another cell and start typing to unselect your copied data. (Clicking on one of the tools in the top menu can work to turn it off as well. In general, this isn't going to be an issue that you notice, but in case it does crop up, Esc is your friend.)

A quick note here, since it came up when I pasted this data into a *Word* document to make sure it would work.

This is what that data looked like in Word:

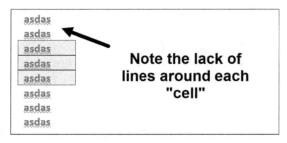

Note the lack of lines around each "cell"

Look carefully at the top two values and the bottom three. See how none of them have a line around them in Word? That's because the default lines that Excel puts around each cell are just there to help you better visualize the separation between the cells. If you actually want your data to copy or print with a border—like the three yellow highlighted cells in the image above—you have to add those borders yourself. (We'll cover how to do that in the formatting chapter.)

I bring this up because in the first Excel for beginners book, I didn't mention that, and then someone sent me a confused email about how tables in Word work (with a built-in border and a set number of cells) versus how tables in Excel work (without borders around cells and no real defined table until you format it to be distinct). So if you're used to working with tables in Word, be a little careful trying to treat data in Excel the same way, because they aren't the same.

Okay. What if you want to move the data altogether, not copy it?

Cut and Paste Data As Is

Cutting data means that you take the contents and formatting that are in a cell or series of cells and you remove it from where it currently is. The cells themselves will remain there, but the contents and formatting of those cells will be gone after you cut those cell contents.

First step, select the cells you want to cut.

Second step, cut. I generally do so using the control shortcut (Ctrl + X), but there is a Cut option in the Clipboard section of the Home tab, as well as a Cut option in the dropdown menu if you right-click.

In Excel, when you cut your selected data, it is still visible in the worksheet. This is different from Word where the text you select and cut will immediately disappear. Which is why in Word you can actually use Cut as another way to delete something, but that doesn't work in Excel.

Third step, go to the top left cell where you want to put the data and paste just the same as you did with copying cells. (Ctrl +V, Enter, or one of the menu options.)

Note that you can only paste data once when you cut it. This is just moving the data from one location to another.

Because you used cut, that will remove the contents and formatting of those cells and place all of it in the new location. Here is a screenshot that's meant to demonstrate the different results between copy and paste:

Rows 1 through 8 are what happens when you copy. The original data was in Column B, I copied and pasted into Column D, and I have the option to paste again because you can still see the dotted green line around Cells B1 through B8.

Rows 11 through 18 are what happens when you cut. The original data was in Column B, I cut and pasted into Column D, and that's it. The data moved completely from Column B to Column D. There is no formatting left in Column B and nothing left for me to move.

With both Copy and Cut you are just taking the contents of the cells not the cells themselves so nothing around the copied or cut cells moves.

Cut or Copy Cells With Formulas

One of the biggest strengths of Excel is the use of formulas and functions, that's why each of my Excel Essentials series has at least one full book devoted to them. And one of the key reasons for that is how formulas in Excel copy.

If you CUT a cell that's using a formula, the formula moves to the new location exactly as is. It continues to reference the exact same cells it referenced before.

If you COPY a cell that's using a formula, the formula adjusts based on how far you moved the data. Copy it down one row and it will reference cells that are also down one row from the original formula.

Let's take a very basic example:

	A	B	C	D	E	F
1	Value 1	Value 2			Value 3	Value 4
2	2	3			121	4
3						
4	Formula	Result			Formula	Value
5	=A2+B2	5		Copy C2	=E2+F2	125
6				Cut C2	=A2+B2	5
7						

In Cell A2 I have entered the value 2. In Cell B2 I have entered the value 3.

In Cell A5 I wrote a very basic formula that adds the value in Cell A2 to the value in Cell B2. That formula is:

$$=A2+B2$$

That says to go to Cell A2 and pull in that value, 2, and then add it to the value found in Cell B2, 3.

Your result is 5, which is displayed in Cell B5.

Take a moment to make sure you're good with that. Cell reference + Cell reference means we add what's in those two cells.

Okay. Now back to copy and cut.

In Cell E5 I COPIED the formula that was in Cell A5 and pasted it in. Because Excel adjusts copied formulas and I had moved the formula over by four columns, each of the cell references also changed by four columns. A2 became E2, B2 became F2. I put different values in Cells E2 and F2 so that it could add up to a different result, 125.

In Cell E6 I CUT the formula that was in Cell A5 (and then typed it back in so I could take the screenshot). Because I cut the formula, it did not change at all. It is still adding A2 to B2.

Before you wonder, "Why does Excel do that?", the adjustment to formulas that Excel makes when you copy is one of its key strengths. Because it lets you write a formula once for the first entry in your data table and then copy that formula down the rest of a column or across the rest of a row. Instead of you having to manually adjust a formula 10,000 times, Excel does it for you in the blink of an eye. It is fantastic. But you need to understand that's what happens to avoid making inadvertent errors.

We will revisit this again in the formulas chapter because there are ways to copy formulas and keep Excel from changing a cell reference that I still want to discuss. But first, let's talk about pasting special.

Copy and Paste Just Values

I mentioned before that I sometimes will copy my data and paste over it to get rid of the formulas. Usually I do this because I manipulated my entries in some way.

For example, say I had an ISBN number (which are used to identify books) that was written as 123-43-1234-0123, but my publishing partner wants the number as 1234312340123, with no dashes. Fortunately, I can use Excel functions to do that rather than have to manually change each one. (I could also probably use Replace, but let's pretend I didn't.)

My temptation after I use a formula to do something like that is to delete the original column of values. Problem is, that when I do that, it ruins my results because those results are the outcome of a formula that references the original column.

So if I don't need my formulas to keep running, I like to get rid of them. The way to do this is to use Paste Special – Values.

The initial steps when using Paste Special – Values are exactly the same. You select your cells, *copy* your values, and select where you want that data to go (which can be the same location that you copied from).

But the next step is to either right-click or use the Paste dropdown menu in the Clipboard section of the Home tab, and then click on the paste option with 123 on the clipboard.

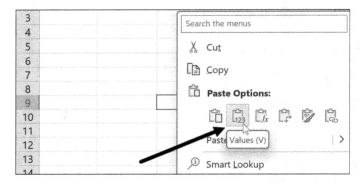

In the image above, I've placed my mouse over it so you can see that it's the "Values" paste option.

In the Paste dropdown it's positioned a little differently:

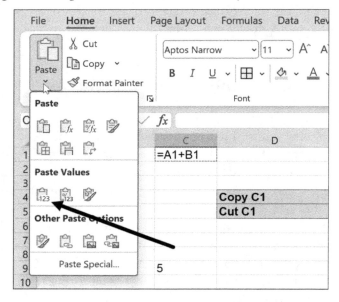

Copy a Column of Data and Paste as a Row or
Copy a Row of Data and Paste as a Column

Another Paste Special option that exists in Excel is to take data that you have in a column and paste it so it's across a row. Or to take data that you have in a row and paste it so that it's down a column.

The Transpose option currently looks like arrows pointing to the right and down in the bottom corner of the clipboard, and as you hold your cursor over that option you should see a preview in the background of what your result will look like:

	2	Amazon	$ 1,234.56	$ 1,135.80		
3	Kobo	$ 2,345.67	$ 2,158.02	
4	Nook	$ 3,456.78	$ 3,180.24	
5	Google	$ 4,567.89	$ 4,202.46	

It is available in the dropdown when you right-click on your selected range, or in the Paste dropdown in the Clipboard section of the Home tab.

You can even do this with a data table, so do both at once. Here's an example:

In Cells A1 through C5 I had a very basic table of data. There were two years of sales results for four vendors.

I selected Cells A1 through C5 and then Pasted Special using the Transpose option into Cell A8. That pasted the values (and formatting) from the table in Cells A1 through C5 into Cells A8 through C12. Note that now the vendor names are across the top and the years are down the left of the table, and the values inside the table also pivoted.

Other Copy-and-Paste-Special Comments

Note that the Paste Special options are only available when you copy. They are not available when you cut your data. So if you want to move the data and change it, it's a two-step process. Change it first, move it second.

As you can see, there are a number of other Paste Special options available in the Paste dropdown menu when you copy cells. I don't think I've ever needed to use any of them, but every tool or function in Excel exists because at some point someone needed it enough for the designers to put in the time to create it. Feel free to experiment and see what they do.

Paste Special – Formatting, for example, might be nice if you have a table of data that is already formatted and need an identical table for new data but don't want to redo all that formatting. You could copy the original table and Paste Special – Formatting to get a blank table with the formatting already in place.

Finally, with each version of Office they like to change the appearance of things. And sometimes it's not quite obvious what something now looks like. So if you ever can't find a paste option you want, click on Paste Special in one of the two dropdown menus. That will bring up the Paste Special dialogue box, which is text-based:

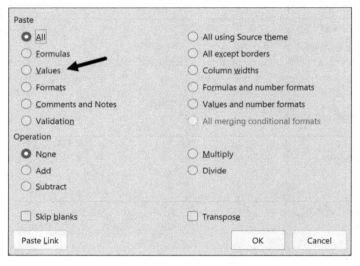

You can then click on the circle next to the option(s) you want and click on OK to apply it.

Copy From Another Program to Excel

One final tip. If you copy text from another program and try to paste into a cell in Excel, Excel will break the text across rows based on where any Enters were. So three paragraphs of text will end up in three cells in an Excel worksheet. If you want all of the text in one cell, double-click on that cell before you paste.

* * *

On to formatting, with one quick detour since the way you plan to use your worksheet will impact how you input and format that data.

A Quick Note on Data Analysis
Versus Data Reporting

In the following chapters we are going to cover how to format your data as well as some basic ways to analyze it. Before we do that, I want to take a quick moment and discuss the difference between data that you use for analysis and data that you use for reporting.

If you want to use your data for analysis—meaning you plan to sort, filter, use formulas, create charts, or create pivot tables with it—there are a handful of best practices to follow.

1. Use one row of your worksheet for your data labels, preferably the top row. (This is the row you can freeze and also the one to use for filtering when we reach that discussion.)

2. List all of your data below that label row in continuous rows with one row that contains all of the data for that entry (customer transaction, for example). DO NOT include subtotals or subheadings, those are for reports. If you want to look at your data using specific groupings, then have a column with that information in it for each row.

3. Standardize as many values as possible.

   Customer A should always be Customer A. An entry like State should not be freeform. You want everyone to enter CO for Colorado not CO, Colorado, Colarado, Colo, etc.

4. Format your data in a way that makes it easier to analyze.

   Specific values and random text are not as easy to analyze as category variables. Where it makes sense to do so, such as customer income for financial professionals, it is better to have five buckets that represent income ranges than list the specific income for each customer. The best way to approach this concept is to think about what you'd do if you were doing this manually. Would it matter that one customer earns $15,234.21 a year and another earns $17,564.32? If not, then find a way to bucket those values.

5. Store your raw data in one place, correct it in another place, analyze it in a third, and report on it in a fourth.

This can be worksheets in the same workbook, but you want to keep the raw data untouched in case you mess up somewhere along the line. And by keeping the intermediate steps, you can sometimes save having to start over.

Here's an example of what I'm talking about in Items 3 and 4 above:

	A	B	C	D	E
1	**Customer Name**	**Customer Feedback**	**Customer Score**		
2	Joe Smith	I really am not happy with you guys.	1		
3	Ming Lin	You are the best.	5	**Standardized Value**	
4	Isabel Rodriguez	I don't even care enough to give my opinion.	3		
5					
6		**Freeform Text**			

This is a data table of feedback from three different customers. One is unhappy, one is pleased, and one really could care less.

You can see that by reading the comments in the freeform text column (Column B). Which is fine to use when you have three customers. But what about 3,000? Or 30,000? Or 300,000? How do you find "good" comments versus "bad" comments?

There are ways that people do that with data analysis, but it's much easier to have values like those in Column C that give that same feedback but in a standardized way. You can see the average rating as easily with 30,000 reviewers as 3.

Do you lose some nuance? Yes, absolutely. And sometimes that's why it's best to capture both.

* * *

What about data for reporting?

In that case, subtotals and subheadings are fine. As are grand totals and special formatting.

A report should be designed in such a way that it's easy for the end user to understand. Expect that data that's prepared for reporting purposes will be printed out. Can it print well? Are there borders? And totals?

Can it be understood just by looking at the printed result? Do the labels and categories make sense to an end-user? Or are the labels still Field1, Field 22, etc.? If you need notes or definitions, are they visible when printed?

This is why data that is formatted for reporting is not good to use for analysis and vice versa. I raise these issues now because if you think about it all ahead of time, you can save yourself a lot of stress and heartache down the road.

Okay, then. Time to learn about formatting.

Formatting

It's all well and good to enter data into Excel. Pretty easy at its core, right, you just click and type. But without formatting your data you can end up with a hideous looking mess that's hard to use. Especially if you want to print anything.

Here, for example, is the print preview for two pages of an imported but unformatted report from one of my vendors:

Title	Author	Units	Publisher I	Currency c	Customer	Customer	Country C	Product T)
A Missing	Aleksa Ba:	3	2.8	USD	3.99	USD	US	EB1
A Dead M:	Aleksa Ba:	1	2.8	USD	3.99	USD	US	EB1
Halloween	Aleksa Ba:	3	0.7	USD	0.99	USD	US	EB1
Excel for E	M.L. Hum	1	385	JPY	550	JPY	JP	EB1
Rider's Re	Alessandr:	1	10.5	USD	14.99	USD	US	EB1
A Buried E	Aleksa Ba:	3	2.8	USD	3.99	USD	US	EB1
A Crazy C	Aleksa Ba:	2	2.8	USD	3.99	USD	US	EB1
Intermedia	M.L. Hum	1	455	JPY	650	JPY	JP	EB1

Pre-Order	Promo Co	ISBN	Apple Ider	Vendor Id	Vendor Of	Begin Dat	End Date	Publisher
			1.49E+09	1.01E+10		11/1/2019	#######	Aleksa Ba:
			1.49E+09	1.01E+10		11/1/2019	#######	Aleksa Ba:
			1.49E+09	1.01E+10		11/1/2019	#######	Aleksa Ba:
			1.49E+09	1.01E+10		11/1/2019	#######	M.L. Hum
			1.49E+09	1.01E+10		11/1/2019	#######	Alessandr:
			1.49E+09	1.01E+10		11/1/2019	#######	Aleksa Ba:
			1.49E+09	1.01E+10		11/1/2019	#######	Aleksa Ba:
			1.49E+09	1.01E+10		11/1/2019	#######	M.L. Hum

There are no lines separating the different columns of data. Text is cut off for a number of columns. Whatever is in that End Date column on the second page isn't even visible because the column isn't wide enough to display it. And both Apple ID and Vendor ID are written in scientific notation.

Taking something like that mess and formatting it before you start working with it is essential. Even if you enter your own data, formatting is essential. You do not want to print most data without borders. And I don't think I've ever created a worksheet where I didn't need to adjust column widths. So this chapter matters. A lot.

And because I expect you to come back to this chapter when you need it, I'm going to present the formatting options alphabetically to make them easier to find later. But first, the basics. There are four main ways to format things in Excel 2024:

The first is by using control shortcuts, such as Ctrl + B for bolding text and Ctrl + I for applying italics to text. There aren't a ton of these I use in Excel, but I do use those two all the time.

The second is going to the Font, Alignment, and Number sections of the Home tab and choosing the option you need from there:

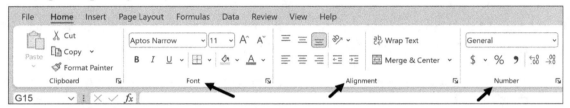

The third, which if you're newer to Excel you may use more than I do, is the mini formatting menu that appears at the top or bottom of the dropdown menu when you right-click after selecting cells in the main workspace:

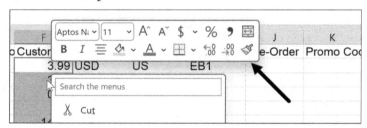

It has a lot of the most common formatting options in it, such as font, font color, font size, fill color, bold, italics, borders, etc.

(You can hold your cursor over each icon to see what it allows you to do if you can't remember.)

The fourth, and least likely to be used, but the one with the most choices, is the Format Cells dialogue box, which you can see on the next page.

To open it, select your cell(s), right-click, and choose Format Cells from the dropdown menu. Or you can click on one of the expansion arrows in the bottom right corner of the Font, Alignment, or Number sections of the Home tab. Note that there are multiple tabs in the Format Cells dialogue box, so you'll need to click over to the one you need.

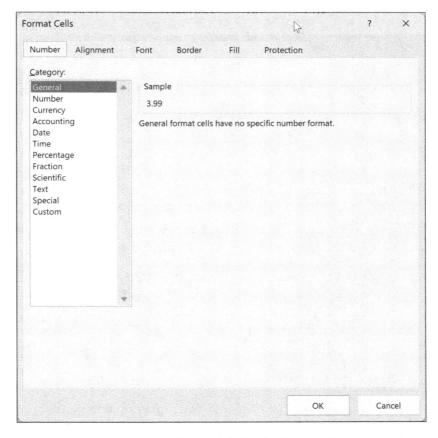

Okay. Let's dive in. Remember, this is listed alphabetically, not from most important to least important.

Align Text Within a Cell

Any text you enter into a cell will by default be aligned to the bottom left side of that cell. Numbers and dates will by default be aligned to the bottom right side of the cell. You can easily see that difference if you increase the height and width of your cells.

You can have your data Top, Middle, or Bottom Aligned, and also Left, Center, or Right Aligned. Which creates nine possible alignments.

Here are examples of each:

A B	C	D	E
Top Left Aligned	Top Center Aligned	Top Right Aligned
Middle Left Aligned	Middle Center Aligned	Middle Right Aligned
Bottom Left Aligned	Bottom Center Aligned	Bottom Right Aligned

To apply the different options, I use the Alignment section of the Home tab. (The mini formatting menu only has the Center option, so is of limited use for this one.)

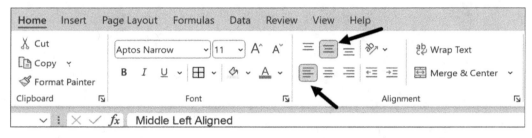

The icons/images for each option show the type of formatting that you're applying.

Note above how the Middle option in the top row shows lines that are all centered top to bottom and the Left option in the second row shows lines that all start on the left edge, for example.

Some formatted numbers or dates may not change when you apply alignment, but text should always change.

You can also use the Alignment tab of the Format Cells dialogue box, which you can see on the next page.

There are dropdowns for Horizontal and Vertical that will contain the relevant options and a few more. The Horizontal dropdown menu, for example, includes additional choices such as Left Indent and Right Indent, and the Vertical dropdown menu includes options for Justify and Distributed.

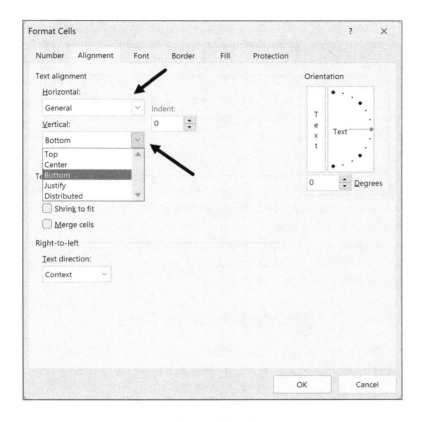

Bold Text

The easiest way to bold the contents of a cell is to click on the cell(s) and use Ctrl + B.

Another option is to select your cell(s) and then click on the bolded B in the Font section of the Home tab or the mini formatting menu.

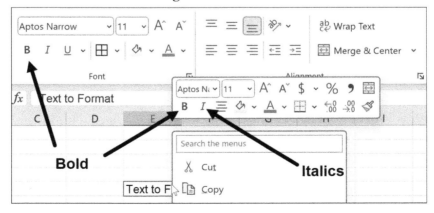

To remove bolding from a cell, you just do the same thing again. Click on the cell and then use Ctrl +B or click on the B in the Font section of the Home tab or the mini formatting menu.

The Font tab in the Format Cells dialogue box has a Font Style set of options that includes Bold and Bold Italic to apply bold to text. Change the style to Regular to remove it.

Sometimes you may want to just bold a single word or set of words within a cell instead of the entire contents of the cell. To do that, double-click on the cell that contains the text you want to bold, select that text, and then apply it. (The mini format menu should automatically appear after you select the text and let up on your mouse, but if it doesn't then the other options are still available.)

If you ever have a cell that has mixed formatting, where part of the text is bolded and part isn't, and you want to apply or remove bold formatting for the entire cell, you may need to use your chosen option more than once.

For example, if you click on a cell that has bolded and unbolded text and use Ctrl + B that is going to apply bold to all of the text in that cell. So to remove bolding from all text in the cell you'd need to use Ctrl + B one more time.

Borders Around Cells

The easiest way to add borders around a cell is to select those cells and then use the borders dropdown menu in the Font section of the Home tab or in the mini formatting menu.

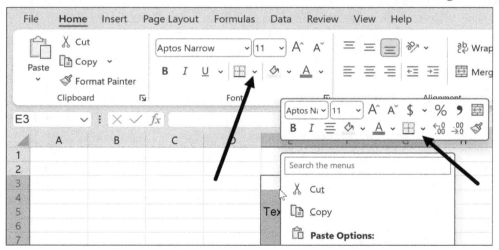

I almost always need to choose from the dropdown menu because I almost never put just a bottom border on a cell, which is the default option.

Click on the arrow next to the current border option to see a full list of choices:

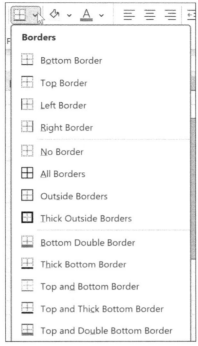

Another option for adding borders is the Draw Border tool in the lower portion of that dropdown menu.

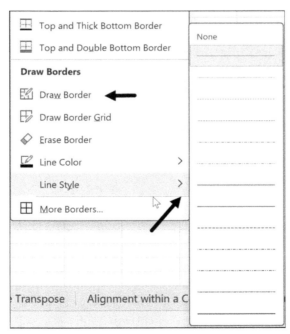

You don't have to select cells first if you use that tool. You can just click on Draw Border and then click and drag in your workspace to put an exterior border around a group of cells.

You can also click on an individual border of an individual cell to put a line on that one border, or click in the middle of a cell and drag a little to put a border around the entire cell. Esc when you're done.

If you don't like the line type or color that Excel uses by default, you can change that in the Draw Borders section of the dropdown menu. In the image above you can see the available Line Style choices, for example.

If you're going to change those attributes, though, you need to change them *before* you apply your lines. Any change you make to line color or line style will only apply to *new* borders not your existing ones.

Finally, you have the option to use the Border tab in the Format Cells dialogue box. That is the only place I know of to get a diagonal line across a cell.

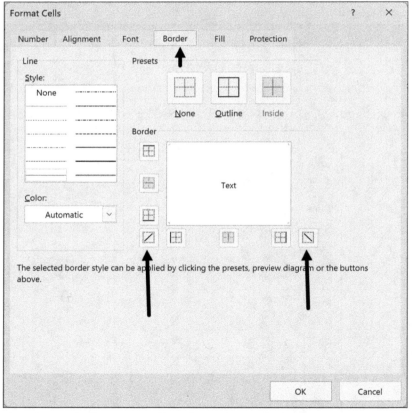

Note that this is a *formatting* line, not a line that corresponds to your text, so if you do this in a cell that has text, you'll get a line that goes from one corner to the opposite corner but your text will still be oriented left to right horizontal by default.

Okay. A few more notes.

When adding a border to cells, I often use a combination of All Borders for all cells in the table and then Thick Outside Borders around the outside edge of the table and the header row.

Now. One tricky thing they've done in recent versions of Excel is make things too subtle. Which means that the border you see on your screen is not the border that will print. See this:

Can you tell in that image that I have two different types of borders applied to those cells? I can't. But when I "print" this to a PDF, this is what I get:

It also looks like this in the print preview in Excel. Note that it changed how my text fits, too. Awful, right? It didn't used to do that.

I don't know which extremely foolish person decided this was a good idea (probably someone who doesn't have to create tables that print from Excel), but it's something to be very aware of when formatting tables in Excel 2024 (or 365). Be sure to look at each table you apply borders to in print preview to make sure the borders look like what you want, and to make sure the text will fit properly, because unfortunately you cannot rely on what's shown in the workspace anymore.

Color a Cell (Fill Color)

You may have noticed that in some of the screenshots I've used a background fill color in a cell like blue or green or orange. I like to do this to distinguish header rows in my tables.

To apply fill color to a cell or cells, select the cell(s), and then go to the Fill Color dropdown in the Font section of the Home tab or in the mini formatting menu:

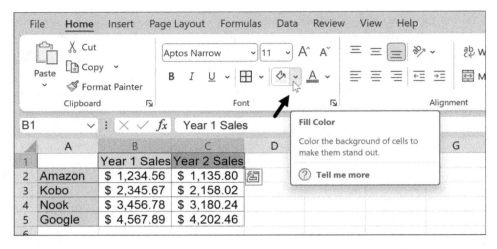

The default is a yellow fill color, which I personally almost never use. Click on the dropdown arrow to see a larger set of color choices:

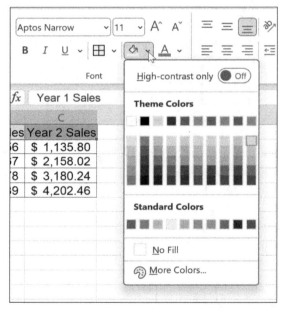

There are seventy different colors to choose from in that dropdown. If one of those works for you, click on it to apply it to your cells.

Note that there is also a No Fill option there in that dropdown that will let you remove any fill that has already been applied.

If you need more color choices, especially for example a specific corporate color, then you can click on the More Colors option. That will bring up the Colors dialogue box which has two tabs, Standard and Custom:

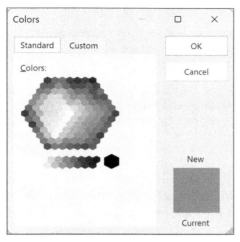 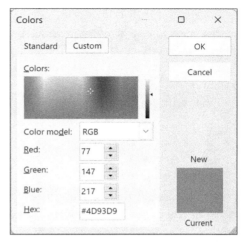

Mine defaulted to the Custom tab when it opened, but let me cover them left to right. The Standard tab has a honeycomb of colors. Click on any spot in the honeycomb to choose that color.

The Custom tab has a rainbow gradient of colors that you can also click on, but where it's more interesting is in the section below that. If you know the exact color you need to use, you can enter the RGB, Hex, or HSL values for that color. (HSL is in the dropdown.) If you have a corporation with a required color palette, they should provide you with those values.

Select your color and then click on OK to apply it.

Note that depending on the color you choose for your background, you may need to then change the font color to keep your text visible. Black on white and white on black are your best contrast choices, but you can also use white or a very light color on a variety of darker backgrounds.

Column Width

As you've seen a couple times already, if your columns aren't wide enough, you may not see all of your text, it will be cut off. For numbers you will see #### in the cell instead of the number. So adjusting column width (and row height) are essential skills to master when working in Excel.

One option is to select all of your columns that have data and then double left click along the border of one of the column names (A, B, C, D, etc.). When that's an available option, the cursor will be a black line with arrows pointing to the left and to the right like in the image on the next page.

	A	B	+ C	D	E	F
1	**Custor**mer	omer **S**core				
2	Joe Sm	I really am	1			
3	Ming Li	You	5	Double Left-Click Along		
		even		Border of Columns B and C		
4	Isabel I	care	3			
5						

If you do that, Excel will automatically adjust your column widths for all of the selected columns to fit the data in each column. This is what I get with the columns in the image above:

	A	B	C	D
1	**Customer Name**	**Customer Feedback**	**Customer Score**	
2	Joe Smith	I really am not happy with you guys.	1	
3	Ming Lin	You are the best.	5	
4	Isabel Rodriguez	I don't even care enough to give my opinion.	3	
5				
6				

Note that the columns are no longer the same width and that the contents in each cell are now fully visible. If you have numeric values, it will normally resize each column to be wide enough to fully display the largest number in the column. With text it's a little trickier because text can be formatted to wrap to the next line, like in Column B. In that case, it will fit the column to the widest text in a single line instead, like it does for Customer Score in Column C.

If you want all of your columns to be the same width, select all of the columns, and then left-click and drag on the right-hand border of one of the column names to get the width you want. If multiple columns are selected, the width you apply to that one column will be applied to all of the selected columns. Drag left to make the columns skinnier, drag right to make them wider.

If you just want to adjust one column, you don't need to select it first, just left-click and drag from the right-hand side of the column name.

(In each of the instances above, your cursor will be that line with arrows on either side when you can do this.)

Another option is to select the column or columns you want to adjust and then right-click and choose Column Width from the dropdown menu. This will bring up the Column Width dialogue box where you can enter an exact numeric value for your desired column width. That width will be applied to all selected columns.

(I don't use that option often because I am a horrible judge of what a width of 50 is compared to 10 so it's too much trial and error for me to bother with, but it is an option.)

Currency Format

You can easily apply formatting to turn an entry like "25" into a currency format like "$25.00".

There are two main choices available in the Number section of the Home tab, Accounting and Currency. Here are examples of both:

No Format		25
Accounting ($)	$	(25.00)
Currency		-$25.00

In the first row, you can see how 25 looks when it's just typed into a cell.

The next line shows the accounting format which you can apply by using the $ sign in either the Number section of the Home tab or the mini formatting menu.

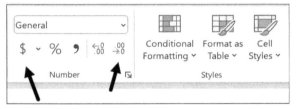

For those of you whose currency symbol is not the dollar sign ($), there is a dropdown next to the $ symbol which includes the British pound, Euro, Chinese Yen, and Swiss Franc symbol.

(This is how it works for me in the U.S. It is possible that versions of Excel sold into different markets will have different defaults or added choices. If the currency you want isn't in either of those lists, click on More Accounting Formats to open the Format Cells dialogue box.)

The final example shows the Currency format. This can be applied by clicking on the dropdown menu in the Number section of the Home tab:

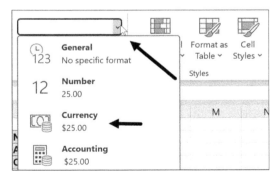

The format will be listed as General by default.

The main difference between the two is where the $ sign is placed and how they are aligned within the cell. For the Accounting format, the currency symbol will be along the left edge of the cell. For the Currency format, the currency symbol will be directly next to the number.

They also treat negative numbers differently. Accounting uses parens, Currency just uses a negative sign.

Accounting	Currency
$ 1.00	$1.00
$ 12.00	$12.00
$ 120.00	$120.00
$ 1,200.00	$1,200.00
$ (1,200.00)	-$1,200.00

If you ever want a currency value but without decimal places, you can use the Decrease Decimal option from the Number section of the Home tab or the mini formatting menu. I pointed to it in the second screenshot in this section. Click on it twice to remove both decimal places.

Also, you can use the Format Cells dialogue box to apply currency formatting. On the Number tab, choose either Currency or Accounting from the left-hand menu. If you choose the Currency format, you can also apply a format that colors negative numbers red. If you choose the Accounting format, the Symbol dropdown menu has a much larger list of currency symbols to choose from.

One final note: Just because you format a value as currency or accounting with two decimal places, that doesn't mean that Excel won't retain the original value behind the scenes and use it in any calculations. So if you have a value of 1.2345 and you format it as currency, it will display as $1.23, but Excel will continue to use 1.2345 in any formulas. (There is a function called ROUND that you can use to convert a number to just two decimal places if that's an issue.)

Date Format

Excel loves to turn entries that look remotely like a date into a date, but often it chooses a date format that I don't like, so this is one I change frequently. For example, if you type "January 1, 1990" into a cell, Excel will immediately display that as 1-Jan-90.

If you type "January 1990" it displays that as Jan-90, and behind the scenes turns it into January 1, 1990. (All dates in Excel are stored as numbers so Excel has to assign a month, day of the month, and year to a date even if you don't.)

To apply date formatting or change the formatting of a date, select the cell(s), go to the dropdown menu in the Number section of the Home tab, and choose Short Date or Long Date:

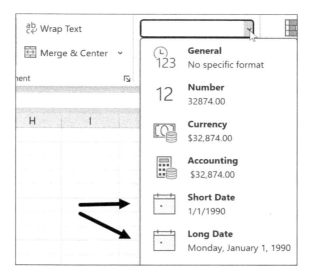

The nice thing about that dropdown is that it gives you a preview of what this particular cell will look like when you apply that formatting.

Now, I like Short Date and usually use it because it's easy, but there are a lot of other date formats I like that aren't shown in that dropdown. In that case, you need to go to the Format Cells dialogue box. The easiest way to get there is to click on the expansion arrow in the bottom right corner of the Number section of the Home tab. You should already be on the Number tab of the Format Text dialogue box. Next, click on Date or Custom.

Here is Date:

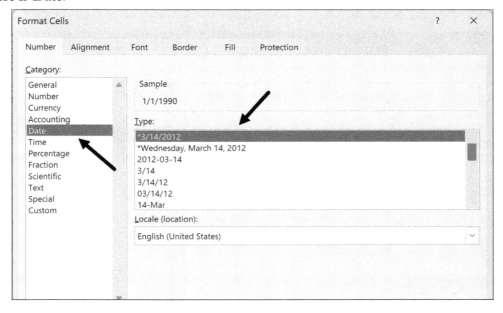

See all those formats there? Just click on the one you want.

If you think your workbook may be used in different countries, pay attention to which date formats adjust for where the user is, and which don't. Also, different countries write month and day of the month in a different order, so some will write January 4, 2020 as 1/4/20 and others will write it as 4/1/20. If you think your audience may cover both of those uses, then don't choose a format where there can be confusion like that. Choose something like 04-Jan-2020 where it's clear what the date is.

A few more comments on dates:

Excel will sometimes get stuck on date formatting. Once a cell gets formatted by Excel as a date it's very stubborn about it. So sometimes you have to clear all formatting or even delete a cell to get it to work for anything but a date in that specific format.

Also, if you enter a two-digit year for a date, like 1/1/20, Excel has rules it applies to decide which century you meant, 1920 or 2020. It's a good practice, which I fail to follow myself, to use a date format that displays the full four-digit year so you can make sure your date is correct.

Finally, if you just enter a date and month (1/1), Excel will automatically assume you meant the date to be in the current year.

Direction of Text

In addition to the basic alignment of your data within a cell, you can also change the direction that text flows.

By default, as you've seen already, text is left to right along a horizontal line. But especially when building a table that you want to print out, you may want to change that. The text direction options are found in the dropdown that's labeled with an angled ab with an arrow under it in the top row of the Alignment section of the Home tab:

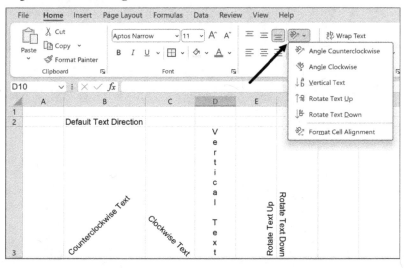

Above you can see how each choice would look in an Excel worksheet. I tend to use that Rotate Text Up option (in Column E) often when building a table with values along the side of a table that need a label. (We'll see an example later.)

Be careful using the clockwise and counterclockwise options, because they change the angle of the cells, too, not just the text in the cell, so if you try to have cells that have clockwise or counterclockwise text in the same row as cells that have "normal" text or are empty, the borders are not going to work.

Here is an example where I applied Counterclockwise Text formatting to six cells in two different rows and put borders around the cells in each row.

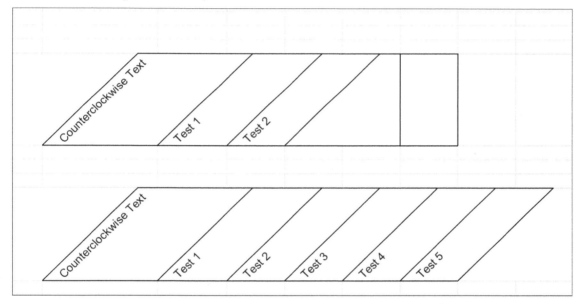

In the first example, only three of those cells have actual text in them. In the second example, all six have text. Note the issues there with the borders when the cells don't have text? So if you use those two settings, it's an all or none deal for that row.

Also, be careful with entering data in rows below that. You can. It works fine. But that last column extends past the column it labels by two more columns. Printed it will look fine, but pay attention to that when you're creating your data table.

If you want more control over the angle of your text, use the Orientation option in the Alignment tab of the Format Cells dialogue box. That will allow you to type in the exact angle you want:

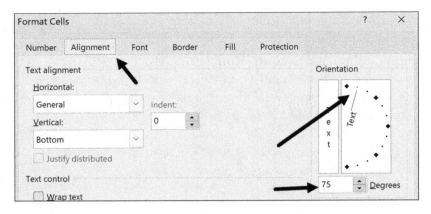

Font

The current default font in Excel is Aptos Narrow. To change that, select your cell(s) or text, and then go to the Font section of the Home tab or the mini formatting menu and use the Font dropdown menu:

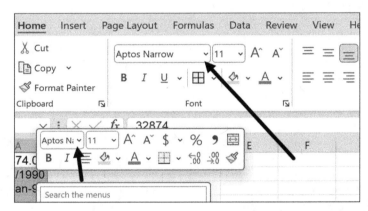

Click on the arrow next to the current font name to see a list of available fonts. Each font listed will be written in that font so you can see what the font looks like when used. On the next page, for example, you can see that Algerian is a very different font from Allura.

Your font list will probably be different from mine. Office offers a large number of fonts for you to use, like Times New Roman, Arial, etc., but I happen to have a lot of other fonts I've purchased. So my list includes all of my available fonts in addition to the ones offered by Office.

To find the font you want, click into that field and start typing and/or use the scroll bars to move through the alphabetical listing.

When you see the font you want, click on it.

If it's displayed in the font box because you started typing the name, hit Enter.

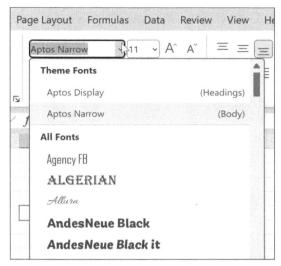

You can also use the Font tab of the Format Cells dialogue box to change the font. There's a listing of all available fonts there as well, but you'll have to use the scroll bars to navigate to the font you want or type out the entire font name to move to that part of the font list.

Font Color

The default color for text in Excel is black, but there will be times when you want to change this. For example, if you use a dark fill color on cells, it's best to then change the text color to white to keep your text legible.

Both the Font section of the Home tab and the mini formatting menu have a dropdown for font color. It will be the letter A above, by default, a red line:

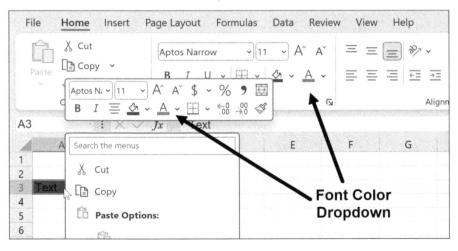

Font Color Dropdown

After you've changed your color at least once during an Excel session, that color under the A will be the last color you used. If you want the color under the A, you can just click on the A.

If you want a different color, click on the dropdown arrow next to the A to see more choices:

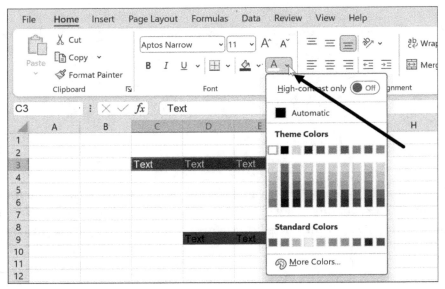

Just like with Fill Color, you'll have 70 choices to choose from in that dropdown, as well as the option to click on More Colors and use a custom color.

In Excel 2024 you have the option in the color dropdown to choose "High-Contrast Only" colors by toggling that option at the top of the dropdown to on. (Click on the word Off to do so.) That will reduce the number of colors you can choose, but it will theoretically ensure that whatever color you do choose will be visible on your current background color.

Here you can see that because I have a dark fill color in the selected cells, Excel is only showing me lighter-colored text options:

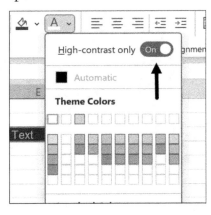

Use your judgment when selecting a color because for me there were still a couple that didn't work well.

To see how a color will look if applied, move your cursor over each option. Click on your choice to apply.

Finally, there is also an option for color on the Font tab of the Format Cells dialogue box.

Font Size

The default font size in Excel is 11 point. If you want bigger or smaller text, you can change that by using the Font Size dropdown menu in the Font section of the Home tab or in the mini formatting menu to pick a new value.

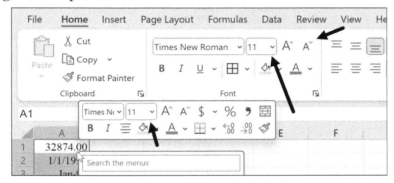

Next to the dropdown menu that lists the current font size are two choices with an A. One has an up arrow; one has a down arrow. Clicking on those will move your font size up or down one spot on the dropdown list of font sizes.

Not every single number is in that list in the dropdown. If you want a different point size, just click into that field and type the value you want. Use Enter ,or click away when you're done.

You can also change the font size in the Format Cells dialogue box.

Italicize Text

You italicize text in the same way you bold text.

Select the cell(s) or text you want to apply your formatting to, and then either use Ctrl + I or click on the slanted I in the Font section of the Home tab or the mini formatting menu.

The Format Cells dialogue box also has an Italic font style option on the Font tab as well as a Bold Italic option.

To remove italics it again works the same as removing bold from text. Select the cell(s) or text, use Ctrl + I or the slanted I symbol. If you select text that is partially formatted as italic and partially not, you may have to do it twice.

Or you can select your text and then use the Format Cells dialogue box to choose the Regular font style.

Merge Cells

There will be times when you want to merge cells together. For example, I will often do this with a header row for a data table. Like in Row 2 of this table:

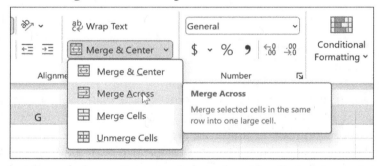

The way to do that is to select the cells you want to merge, go to the Alignment section of the Home tab, and use the Merge & Center dropdown menu:

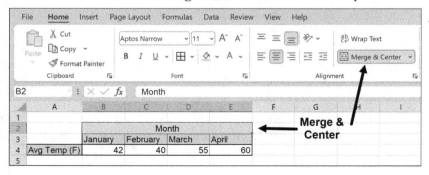

Merge Cells is what I used above. It merged the selected cells but kept the text left-aligned. You can use Merge Cells across any number of rows or columns and it will merge all of the selected cells into one single cell.

Merge & Center may have been the better option to use above, because it not only merges the selected cells but it also will Center align the text across that newly-created cell:

Merge & Center is also an option in the top right corner of the mini formatting menu.

Merge Across is nice when you have multiple rows where you want to merge across columns, but still keep the rows separate. You can select an entire range, say Cells B2 through E4, and Excel will merge B2 to E2, B3 to E3, and B4 to E4 separately. (You'll see some examples of that in these books.)

Use a bit of caution if you already have data in the cells you're trying to merge. Excel will keep whatever is in the top left cell of the selected range and delete the rest. You should see a warning message if that's going to happen.

Unmerging the cells (which is another option in that dropdown) will not bring back the lost contents of those cells. You need to Undo to get the other text back.

Also, If you have cells that were already merged, clicking on one of the merge options will unmerge them.

One final tip: Merged cells should be reserved for when you are creating a report using finalized data, not for a data table that you intend to do data analysis on. Merged cells don't tend to play well with pivot tables, filtering, sorting, or some formulas. If you do use a formula that references merged cells, the cell reference will be the top left corner of the merged cell.

You can see the cell reference to use for a merged cell to the left of the formula bar when you click on the merged cell.

Number Format

If you know going in that you're dealing with a type of number where Excel is difficult (ISBNs, zip codes, etc.), it's best to apply the formatting to those cells before you add your data.

To apply a generic number format to your cells, select the cell(s) that you want to format (including an entire column, if needed), and go to the Number section of the Home tab.

Your first option is to use the comma under the dropdown menu or in the mini formatting menu to apply the Comma Style, which has two decimal places and uses commas to separate the hundreds:

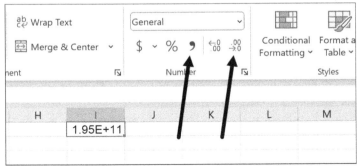

I often don't want decimal places, so will then use the Decrease Decimal option twice to remove them. (You can see the revised result below.)

Another option is to use the dropdown menu in the Number section of the Home tab, which is usually showing as "General" by default, to choose a format:

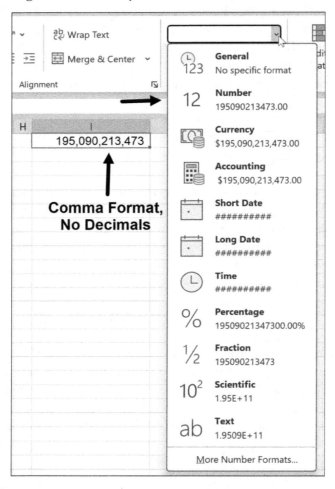

If you have values in the selected cell(s) already, Excel will show you in that dropdown an example of what that value will look like if that format is applied.

A few cautions about numbers in Excel. If you have a large number, like an ISBN number which is fifteen digits, Excel will convert that to scientific notation on you. So if your number looks something like 1.23E+09, that's what's happening

Also, Excel will remove the zero at the start of numbers. This is a problem for zip codes, for example, some of which start with a zero. Since you don't need to do calculations with zip codes, one option is to treat them as text and enter with a single quote mark to make Excel leave those entries as is. The other option is to go to the Number tab of the Format Cells dialogue box, which has a Special format category that includes formats for zip codes.

It also has formats for phone numbers or social security numbers, at least for the United States. Click on each option to see a sample in the dialogue box. Click OK to apply that format to your selected cell(s).

Percent Format

To format numbers as a percentage, select the cell(s) you want to format, and click on the % sign in the Number section of the Home tab or in the mini formatting menu.

Excel is weird but logical with percentages. If the value you're formatting is a decimal (.25) it will convert it to a percentage "normally". In math .25 is the same as 25%.

If the number is a whole number (25), then Excel also adds two zeros at the end and a percentage symbol. So you get 2500%. Perfectly logical when you think about it, but often not expected if you aren't the type of person who thinks mathematically. Which means that if you have values like 25 that are meant to stand for 25%, you need to divide those values by 100 to get them to work with the percentage setting in Excel.

Row Height

Row Height works much like Column Width. Left-click and drag on the line below a row number to adjust the row height manually. You can also double left-click on the line below a row number to resize the row to its contents.

Select multiple rows and use the line below one of the selected rows to adjust multiple rows at once. You can also right-click and choose Row Height from the dropdown menu and then input a specific value.

There is a maximum row height that Excel will adjust to. It is, according to the error message I just got, 409. I have run into this as an issue in the past when I was using Excel for a text-heavy analysis. I had more text than Excel could display in my cell. So if you use Excel for something that involves lots of text in one cell, be aware that it is possible to have your text cut off at the bottom of the cell, and therefore not fully visible. (You can overcome this issue to some extent by widening your columns, but even doing that isn't always enough.)

Underline Text

I underline text far less in Excel than in Word, but it can be needed at times. A basic underline can be applied by selecting the cell(s) or text you want to underline, and then using Ctrl + U or clicking on the U with an underline in the Font section of the Home tab.

If you use the dropdown arrow for the U in the Font section of the Home tab, there is also a double-underline option, which is used in accounting.

In the Font tab of the Format Cells dialogue box there is also an Underline dropdown. It includes Single, Double, Single Accounting, and Double Accounting choices.

To remove an underline, use Ctrl + U again or the U in the Font section of the Home tab. If you applied an underline format other than Single, you will likely have to do that twice because the first time will convert the underline to a single underline. Another option is to change the underline dropdown in the Font tab of the Format Cells dialogue box to None.

Wrap Text

To wrap text, select your cell(s), go to the Alignment section of the Home tab, and click on Wrap Text. (To remove it, just click on the option again.)

Wrap Text is also an option in the Alignment tab of the Format Cells dialogue box.

Why use this? Because by default, text in a cell is going to be on one line. Even if the column of that cell isn't wide enough to display the full text, the text will be visible if that is the only text in that row. But as soon as you put data in a cell to the right, the text will stop at that next cell. Here is an example:

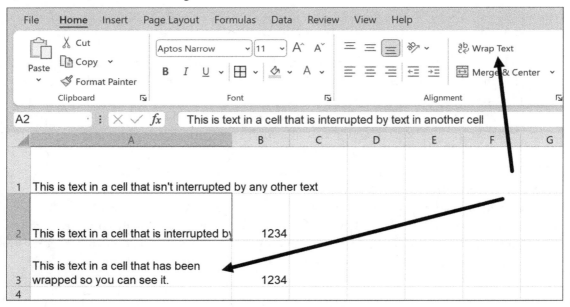

Row 1 has text in Cell A1 but no other text in any cell in the row. You can read the full text even though it stretches to Column C.

Row 2 has text in Cell A2 and a number in Cell B2. The text in Cell A2—which you can still see completely in the formula bar when I click on Cell A2—is cut off at the point where Cell B2 starts.

The way to keep text visible in that situation is to apply Wrap Text. I've done that in Cell A3. Now when the text in Cell A3 reaches Cell B3 it doesn't disappear, it wraps to the next line.

* * *

Before we move on, I want to cover two more formatting tricks.

Copy Formatting

The Format Painter, seen in the Clipboard section of the Home tab or in the mini formatting menu, allows you to take all of the formatting from one cell or range of cells, and apply it to another cell or range of cells.

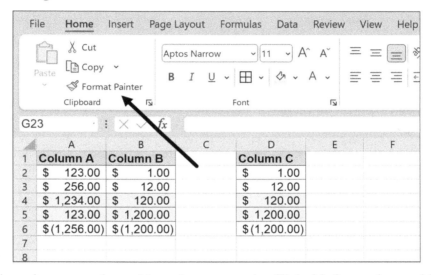

Say you add a column to a data table and you want the fill, bold, font color, and borders that you were using on all of the other columns in that table to apply to the new column. Easy enough to select an existing column that has your formatting, and then use the format painter to transfer that over to the new column, like I've done above.

The first step in using the tool, is to select the range of cells that have your formatting in them. This can be a cell, a row, a column, or even a series of cells, rows, or columns.

Next, click on the Format Painter in the Clipboard section of the Home tab. (Double-click if you want to use that formatting in more than one location that will require you to select cells more than once..)

Finally, select the cell(s) where you want to apply the formatting.

If you want to apply, for example, the formatting of one column to the three columns next to it, you would select that first column, click on the Format Painter, and then select all three of those columns in the last step. As you can see in the image above, it will apply the formatting of different cells in that range to the selected range, so we have cells highlighted yellow in the exact same spot in each column.

If you do double-click on the Format Painter to use it in more than one location, use Esc when you're done to turn it off.

Be aware that ALL of your formatting will transfer.

Also be careful using this tool, because it will apply the formatting to wherever you move next. So if you select a range of cells and click on the Format Painter and then try to arrow over, the Format Painter will apply the selected formatting to that next cell. Best practice is to always click to select the cells where you want to apply that formatting.

Remember with this one that Undo (Ctrl + Z) is your friend if you apply formatting to the wrong range of cells. Just be sure to use Esc to start over if you do need to undo.

Clear Formatting

To clear formatting from cell(s), go to the Editing section of the Home tab, click on the dropdown for Clear, and choose Clear Formats.

If you use Clear All, that will also delete the contents in the selected cell(s) at the same time.

This can be useful when Excel stubbornly decides to format a cell as a date and won't stop trying to do so.

It's also useful when you have borders or other formatting that extend beyond the boundaries of your data and you want to remove it. For example, I recently had a program that would export data which was in maybe fifty rows, but put borders around all cells in those columns for all 1,048,576 rows of the worksheet.

I was able to select the first row that didn't contain data, use Shift + Ctrl + the down arrow key to select the remaining rows in the worksheet, and then use the Clear Format option to remove those borders.

Analyze Data

This chapter is going to cover three different ways to analyze your data: sorting, filtering, and some basic math. You can do a lot with just those three, which is why I'm covering them in this book. If this doesn't feel like enough, the remainder of the books in this series cover additional analysis tools such as charts, pivot tables (officially written as PivotTables), conditional formatting, and more advanced formulas and functions.

To get started, let me show you the first rows of the data we're going to work with:

	A	B	C	D	E	F	G
1	Royalty Date	Author Name	Marketplace	Transaction Type	Net Units Sold	Royalty	Currency
2	2021-01-31	Author A	Amazon.com	Standard	1	5.70	USD
3	2021-01-31	Author B	Amazon.com.au	Standard	1	5.03	AUD
4	2021-01-31	Author C	Amazon.com	Free - Price Match	65	0.00	USD
5	2021-01-31	Author D	Amazon.com	Standard	1	2.76	USD
6	2021-01-31	Author C	Amazon.fr	Free - Price Match	1	0.00	EUR
7	2021-01-31	Author C	Amazon.ca	Free - Price Match	3	0.00	CAD
8	2021-01-31	Author A	Amazon.com	Standard	1	5.83	USD
9	2021-01-31	Author C	Amazon.de	Free - Price Match	3	0.00	EUR
10	2021-01-31	Author A	Amazon.com	Standard	1	1.75	USD
11	2021-01-31	Author A	Amazon.com	Standard	1	2.74	USD
12	2021-01-31	Author A	Amazon.com	Standard	1	3.12	USD
13	2021-01-31	Author D	Amazon.com	Standard	2	5.52	USD
14	2021-01-31	Author D	Amazon.com	Standard	1	2.76	USD
15	2021-01-31	Author F	Amazon.com	Free - Price Match	1	0.00	USD
16	2021-01-31	Author A	Amazon.co.uk	Standard	1	2.72	GBP
17	2021-01-31	Author A	Amazon.com	Standard	1	2.80	USD
18	2021-01-31	Author C	Amazon.com	Free - Price Match	5	0.00	USD

This is sales data for a variety of authors and book titles that shows date of sale, author, where sold, transaction type, number of units sold, amount earned, and currency it was earned in. There are 631 total entries in this data table.

Not pretty, but it doesn't need to be. It just needs to be formatted in a way that works for sorting, filtering, and formulas as we discussed before.

Look At Your Data

Before you start running any analysis on your data, stop for a moment and look at what you have. Understand what it's telling you.

For example, Column G of this data is Currency, and you can see that there are different values in that column: USD, AUD, EUR, CAD, etc. That tells me that I can't just add the values in Column F to get a total sales value. 1 USD is not equivalent to 1 AUD, is not equivalent to 1 CAD.

Another thing you want to do is look at your various columns, and make sure they are formatted the way they should be. For example, Columns E and F are my number columns. Do they behave that way in Excel?

Looking at Cells E2 through E4 I know they should add up to 67 if Excel treats those values as numbers.

To make sure that Excel does see those values as numbers, I can select those cells, and then look in the bottom right corner of the worksheet.

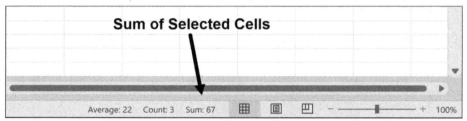

Excel is showing a Sum and an Average for the values in those cells. That means it is treating them as numeric values. If Excel didn't think those were numbers, like in the image below, then it would just give me a count:

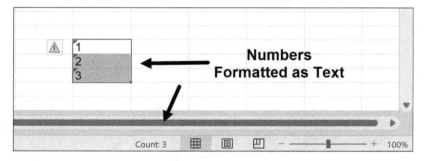

Another way to know you have an issue, is that Excel sometimes flags numbers formatted as text with a green triangle in the top left corner of the cell, as you can see in the image above.

You'll see a caution triangle, like in the image above, when the cells are selected.

Hold your mouse over the caution triangle to see a dropdown arrow. Left-click on the arrow, and you'll see a dropdown menu that shows the reason Excel flagged those cells:

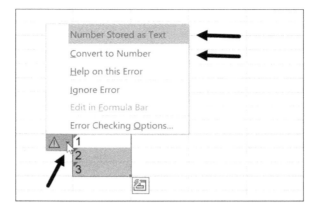

For example, the top line in this example shows "Number Stored as Text". If I want to convert those numbers from text to numbers, I can just click on Convert to Number in that dropdown and all selected cells will convert.

Another thing you want to do with your data before you start, is check for blank lines and blank columns. It is best to remove those if at all possible. At least have the entries in the first row and first column of your data table be continuous. It will make your life easier.

Also, make sure there is just one line per data entry. For example, back in the day Amazon would send sales reports like the one above, but instead of having Marketplace in Column C, they'd put a blank row, and then a row with Marketplace by itself, and then list all transactions for that marketplace below it. Great for a report of sales by marketplace. Awful for a report where you intend to do any sort of analysis.

You do not want breaks for subtotals or subcategories in your data. Convert anything like that into a column that includes those values for each line.

Okay. From here on out, I am going to assume you have good data to work with. First up, filtering.

Filter Data

Filtering lets you take a large data table and narrow down which rows of data are visible, based upon the criteria you choose. So for our sample data, I could use filtering to just look at sales by Author A in the Amazon.de marketplace. Or sales by Authors A, B, and C with a Standard transaction type where the Royalty amount is over 5.00 and the Currency is AUD.

Older versions of Excel were much more limited in terms of how many filter criteria you could apply at once, but Excel 2024 really is not. It's just something to keep in mind if you ever deal with someone with an older version of Excel. (I recommend turning filtering off before you close the file in those situations.)

Okay, first step, how to turn on filtering.

Turn On or Turn Off Filtering

To turn on filtering of your data, click into one of the cells in the top row of your data table, go to the Editing section of the Home tab, click on the Sort & Filter dropdown, and choose Filter.

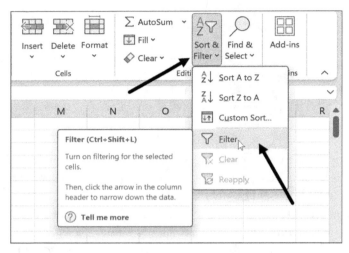

You can see here that Filter also has a control shortcut (Ctrl + Shift + L). That is one I do not have memorized, but I point it out because it could be a useful one to learn, especially since in more recent versions of Excel, I've noticed weird formatting issues with column widths when I have filtering applied to a range of cells. If you ever run into that, turn off filtering, format the cells, and then turn it back on.

To turn filtering off you can just select Filter in the dropdown menu of the Editing section of the Home tab again, or use the Ctrl shortcut.

Another option for turning on filtering, is to right-click on a cell in the data table where you want to filter, go to Filter in the dropdown menu, and then choose your filtering option from there. In that case, it's best to right-click on a cell that meets one of your filter criteria, because it's set up to automatically filter for you based on your selection:

Above you can see that there are options in that dropdown to immediately filter by the selected cell's value, color, font color, or icon.

If you right-click and use the clear filter option that you can see there, that removes the filter for that column, but it leaves filtering in place.

You can also clear filtering from the dropdown menu in the Editing section of the Home tab, by choosing the Clear option, but that will clear filters from all of the columns in the table.

When you turn on filtering, Excel will add little dropdown arrows to every single cell in what it perceives to be the header row of your data table:

	A	B	C	D	E	F	G	H	I
1	Royalty Dat ▼	Author Name ▼	Marketplace ▼	Transaction Ty ▼	Net Units So ▼	Royalty ▼	Currency ▼		Converted Currency
2	2021-01-31	Author A	Amazon.com	Standard	1	5.70	USD		$5.70
3	2021-01-31	Author B	Amazon.com.au	Standard	1	5.03	AUD		$0.00
4	2021-01-31	Author C	Amazon.com	Free - Price Match	65	0.00	USD		$0.00
5	2021-01-31	Author D	Amazon.com	Standard	1	2.76	USD		$2.76
6	2021-01-31	Author C	Amazon.fr	Free - Price Match	1	0.00	EUR	**Filter**	$0.00
7	2021-01-31	Author C	Amazon.ca	Free - Price Match	3	0.00	CAD	**Dropdown**	$0.00
8	2021-01-31	Author A	Amazon.com	Standard	1	5.83	USD	**Arrows**	$5.83
9	2021-01-31	Author C	Amazon.de	Free - Price Match	3	0.00	EUR		$0.00

Note that Column I does not have a dropdown arrow. That's because there was a gap between Columns A through G and Column I, so Excel didn't think Column I was part of the table. (This is why it's best to remove blank columns and rows, so that doesn't happen.)

If I wanted to filter using Column I, I'd need to turn off filtering, and then either click on Column I and turn it on again for just Column I, or delete that blank column and turn it back on for all of my columns.

Another option, if you don't have empty rows at the top of your worksheet, is to Select All or select all of the columns you want to include, before you turn on filtering. Doing it that way would include Columns A through I. (If you try that with data that doesn't start in Row 1, the filters apply in Row 1 not at the top of your data table.)

Another way to apply or remove filtering, is by using the Filter option in the Sort & Filter section of the Data tab.

Filter Dropdown Menu

Click on a filter dropdown arrow to see the options for that column. (An example for Author Name in Column B is on the next page.)

There are three main sections in the dropdown menu. The top section allows for sorting. I never sort data this way, so I'm going to skip it.

The next section allows you to clear a filter from that column, if one is in place, as well as filter by color or by a list of criteria specific to the data type in that column.

The final section lets you choose specific values to include or exclude, and includes a search option.

Your options in each section are going to depend on the type of data Excel thinks is in that column. Text, numbers, and dates are each treated differently.

Author Name is a text field, so the sort below is an A to Z sort, and the values in the bottom section are the unique author names that appear in that column.

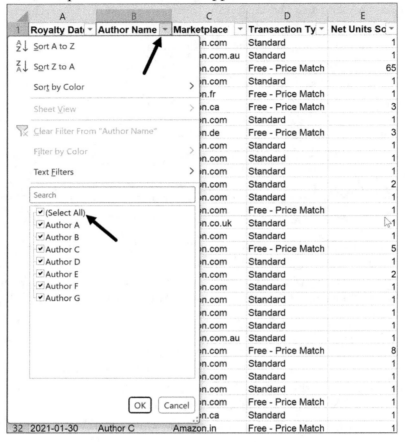

Here are the Text Filter options available in the middle section:

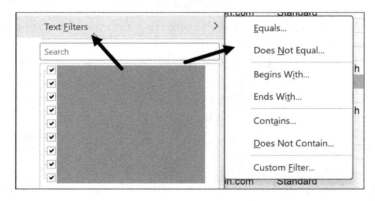

You can choose to look for text that equals, does not equal, begins with, ends with, contains, or does not contain specified text.

For example, one of my vendors used to report sales I had through Overdrive by adding that to the end of the book title. I could filter sales at Overdrive using a "contains" filter, or exclude them with a "does not contain" filter.

For numbers, the bottom section will still list unique values, and you'll have a set of Number Filters options instead:

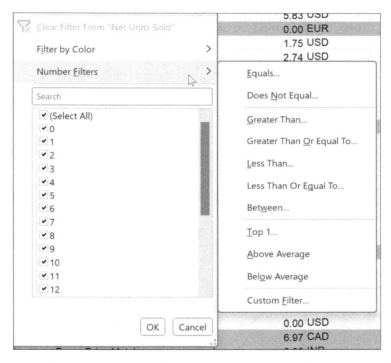

The Numbers Filters choices are equals, does not equal, greater than, greater than or equal to, less than, less than or equal to, between, Top X, Above Average, Below Average, and custom. Custom lets you apply two criteria at once.

Finally, dates, as you can see on the next page, show differently in the bottom section and have their own Date Filters options.

In the bottom section, there are plus signs (+) next to each year and month that you can click to expand the results to see the detail entries.

If a list is expanded, there will be a minus sign (-) that you can click on to collapse the details.

In the image on the next page, I've expanded year (which only has January entries below it), but collapsed month, so you can see both at once.

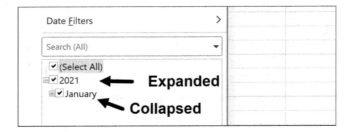

In the secondary dropdown for Date Filters, you can choose Equals, Before, After, Between, and then a large number of options related to the week, month, quarter, or year.

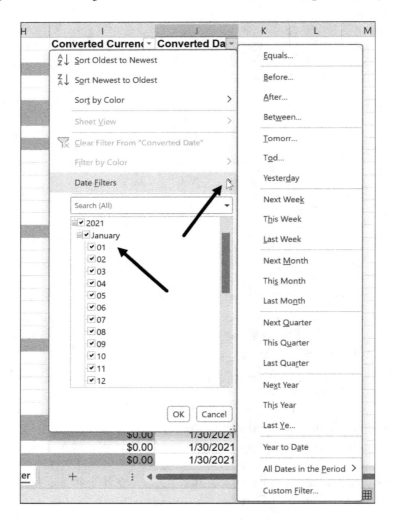

Filtering

There are three primary ways to filter. You can filter by color, by criteria, or by making a specific choice of which values to show.

Let's start with filter by color. I tend to be one of those people who will color the text red if something looks weird, or add fill color to a cell to mark it in some way. If you do that, you can then use the Filter By Color secondary dropdown to see just those colored entries:

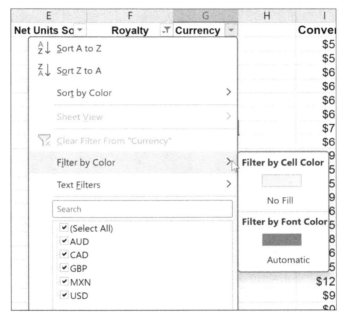

In the image above, you can see that I have entries in that column that are highlighted yellow, as well as entries that have red text. All I have to do is click on the yellow or red in that secondary menu, to narrow my results down to just those values.

Or I can choose No Fill or Automatic color (which just means black for most people) to exclude those entries.

If I were using multiple font or fill colors, all of the colors I was using would show as options in that secondary dropdown menu.

The only drawback on this one, is that you can only filter by one color at a time. So I can filter by one font color or by one fill color, but I can't choose multiple font colors, multiple fill colors, or a combination of a specific font and fill color.

If you're going to take advantage of this, keep that in mind when choosing what to color.

The next filter option is that secondary dropdown list of Text, Number, or Date Filters. I use this one most with numbers.

Here is the dialogue box you'll see if you choose Greater Than or Equal To, for example:

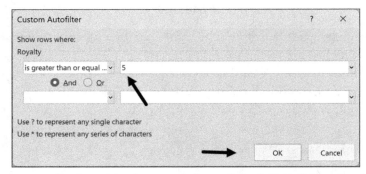

Enter the value you want in the white box, and then click OK. I did so for the Net Units Sold column, and now have all entries where that value is 5 or more:

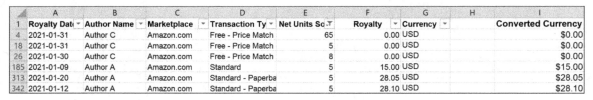

(Note that even though Converted Currency is not a column I can filter on right now, filters apply to an entire row, so the values in that column still correspond to the values in the data table.)

Finally, we have the checkbox and search options at the bottom.

Let's go back to our Author field listing:

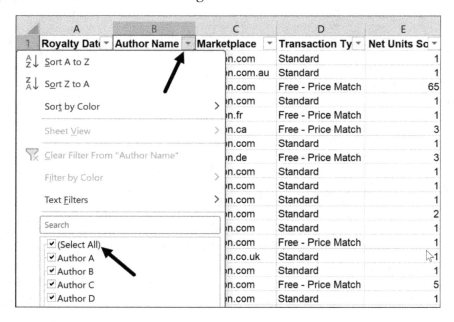

If I want only Author A, the easiest way to get that is to click on the Select All box at the top to unselect all of the entries, and then click on Author A. I can then click on OK to apply. And here we are:

	A	B	C	D	E	F	G
1	Royalty Dat ▾	Author Name ⊤	Marketplace ▾	Transaction Ty ▾	Net Units So ▾	Royalty ▾	Currency ▾
2	2021-01-31	Author A	Amazon.com	Standard	1	5.70	USD
8	2021-01-31	Author A	Amazon.com	Standard	1	5.83	USD
10	2021-01-31	Author A	Amazon.com	Standard	1	1.75	USD
11	2021-01-31	Author A	Amazon.com	Standard	1	2.74	USD
12	2021-01-31	Author A	Amazon.com	Standard	1	3.12	USD
16	2021-01-31	Author A	Amazon.co.uk	Standard	1	2.72	GBP
17	2021-01-31	Author A	Amazon.com	Standard	1	2.80	USD
21	2021-01-31	Author A	Amazon.com	Standard	1	1.97	USD

If I wanted Authors A and B, I'd unselect all and check the boxes next to both Author A and Author B.

This works the same for numbers and dates, too. Select All to deselect and then make your choices. For dates, if you want more than one day, month, or year, just expand that section to check the appropriate boxes.

If your list of unique text values is very long, you can use the search box to narrow down the listed results. As you type in your text, the list of values that you can check or uncheck will narrow down to just those that match what you've typed.

Here I've clicked on filter for the Marketplace column and started to type "fr" for France:

	A	B	C	D
1	Royalty Dat ▾	Author Name ⊤	Marketplace ▾	Transaction Ty ▾
2	2021-	A↓Z Sort A to Z		Standard
8	2021-			Standard
10	2021-	Z↓A Sort Z to A		Standard
11	2021-			Standard
12	2021-	Sort by Color ＞		Standard
16	2021-			Standard
17	2021-	Sheet View ＞		Standard
21	2021-	▽✕ Clear Filter From "Marketplace"		Standard
22	2021-			Standard
23	2021-	Filter by Color ＞		Standard
24	2021-			Standard
28	2021-	Text Filters ＞		Standard
31	2021-	fr ✕		Standard
35	2021-	☑ (Select All Search Results)		Standard
36	2021-	☐ Add current selection to filter		Standard
37	2021-	☑ Amazon.fr		Standard
38	2021-			Standard

You can see it narrowed it down to the one result that contains "fr". I can then click OK and it will apply that filter.

I find that search doesn't work as well with numbers or dates. But the values listed in that section are in numeric and date order, so it's relatively easy to use the scroll bars on the sides to find the values I want. I just have to remember to uncheck Select All first.

Appearance When Data Is Filtered

When your data is filtered, the row numbers will be colored blue. This means there are rows that have been filtered out.

You will also be able to see that the row numbers skip. Your rows will go from Row 2 to Row 8, for example, if the criteria you applied excludes the values in Rows 3 through 7.

Another thing to note is that the dropdown arrow for a column where a filter has been applied will change to a funnel. Since you can filter by more than one column at a time, you may see more than one funnel:

	A	B	C	D	E
1	Royalty Dat ▼	Author Name .T	Marketplace ▼	Transaction Ty .T	Net Units So ▼
2	2021-01-31	Author A	Amazon.com	Standard	1
8	2021-01-31	Author A	Amazon.com	Standard	1
10	2021-01-31	Author A	Amazon.com	Standard	1
11	2021-01-31	Author A	Amazon.com	Standard	1
12	2021-01-31	Author A	Amazon.com	Standard	1
16	2021-01-31	Author A	Amazon.co.uk	Standard	1
17	2021-01-31	Author A	Amazon.com	Standard	1

Finally, when you filter your data, you can look in the bottom left corner to see how many entries out of your total lines of data met your filter criteria:

51	2021-01-28	Author A	Amazon.it	Standard	1
53	2021-01-28	Author A	Amazon.com	Standard	1
54	2021-01-27	Author A	Amazon.co.uk	Standard	1
55	2021-01-27	Author A	Amazon.com	Standard	2
56	2021-01-27	Author A	Amazon.com	Standard	2

| < | ••• | Currency Format | Dates | Font Color | Merge | Sheet4 | F |

Ready   532 of 631 records found   Accessibility: Investigate

Here it says 532 of 631 records found. That is an easy way to get a count of records that meet your filter criteria.

Also, if you look at that number of total records and it is less than you think it should be, check your data for blank rows, because Excel may have stopped at that point rather than including all of your data.

You can also try to unapply and reapply your filters if you added new data to the bottom of your table and think Excel didn't incorporate it into the filtered data table.

(Ctrl + the down arrow will take you to the last populated field in a data range. That row number minus 1 should be your number of total records if your data starts in Row 1 and there are no blank rows.)

Final Thoughts

I recommend not leaving filtering on. We already discussed that it can be a compatibility issue with older versions of Excel, but also, you don't want to share information that you hadn't planned on sharing. I once had someone provide me a worksheet that was meant to show me our client billing for one specific project but they'd done it using filters. I turned off the filter and was able to see all of our client billing for the entire year.

Also, copy and paste when data is filtered can be tricky. And I honestly think it's gotten worse over the years. Only ever copy and paste one value at a time in your table when your data is filtered.

You can paste one value to multiple cells in a column, no problem, but if you copy three rows of values and try to paste those into another column in your table, they won't paste into the rows you can see, they will paste into the next three rows, even if two of those rows are currently filtered out.

Let's look at an example. Here I have a filtered data table. You can see that it jumps from Row 2 to Row 8 to Row 31 to Row 49.

	A	B	C	D	Net
1	Royalty Date ⌄	Author Name ⌄	Marketplace ⌄	Transaction Ty ⌄	
2	2021-01-31	Author A	2021-01-31	Standard	
8	2021-01-31	Author A	Amazon.com	Standard	
31	2021-01-30	Author A	Amazon.ca	Standard	
49	2021-01-28	Author A	Amazon.com	Standard	
55	2021-01-27	Author A	Amazon.com	Standard	
56	2021-01-27	Author A	Amazon.com	Standard	
60	2021-01-27	Author A	Amazon.co.uk	Standard	

I copied the values in Cells A2 through A31, and pasted them in Cell C2. Easy enough to do. Excel lets you do that no problem. This is great if you want to paste into a new worksheet. But note that you can only see one of the dates I copied.

Why is that? Because the values copied to Cells C2 through C5 even though Cells C3 through C5 weren't visible at the time:

	A	B	C	D	E
1	Royalty Date ⌄	Author Name ⌄	Marketplace ⌄	Transaction Ty ⌄	Net Units So ⌄
2	2021-01-31	Author A	2021-01-31	Standard	1
3	2021-01-31	Author B	2021-01-31	Standard	1
4	2021-01-31	Author C	2021-01-30	Free - Price Match	65
5	2021-01-31	Author D	2021-01-28	Standard	1
6	2021-01-31	Author C	Amazon.fr	Free - Price Match	1
7	2021-01-31	Author C	Amazon.ca	Free - Price Match	3
8	2021-01-31	Author A	Amazon.com	Standard	1

This is an issue I run into all the time using filtering. So be very careful of this. You can copy *one* value and paste it into multiple cells in a filtered table, no problem, but you cannot copy multiple values and paste them successfully into a filtered table.

Sort Data

Now let's talk about sorting. Sorting data lets you put your entries into an order that makes better sense.

For example, in my day job I deal with a lot of financial records. So I might enter data from one bank statement and then another, but at the end of the day I want all of the entries sorted in date order, so I can see what happened in those accounts over time.

Before we start, you need to be careful with sorting, because you can "break your data" very easily. By break your data, what I mean is that your different columns of data are not inherently linked. So when you sort your data, if you fail to include all of the relevant columns, then you can break the relationship between the columns you did sort and the remaining columns.

Let's look at an example. Here I've added fill color to my data for all transactions that are not on Amazon.com:

	A	B	C	D	E	F	G	H	I
1	Royalty Date	Author Name	Marketplace	Transaction Ty	Net Units So	Royalty	Currency		Converted
2	2021-01-31	Author A	Amazon.com	Standard	1	5.70	USD		$5.70
3	2021-01-31	Author B	Amazon.com.au	Standard	1	5.03	AUD		$0.00
4	2021-01-31	Author C	Amazon.com	Free - Price Match	65	0.00	USD		$0.00
5	2021-01-31	Author D	Amazon.com	Standard	1	2.76	USD		$2.76
6	2021-01-31	Author C	Amazon.fr	Free - Price Match	1	0.00	EUR		$0.00
7	2021-01-31	Author C	Amazon.ca	Free - Price Match	3	0.00	CAD		$0.00
8	2021-01-31	Author A	Amazon.com	Standard	1	5.83	USD		$5.83
9	2021-01-31	Author C	Amazon.de	Free - Price Match	3	0.00	EUR		$0.00

You can see that each row is either all blue or all not blue.

Now what if I want to sort on number of units in Column E, but I only sort on that column? See what happens:

	A	B	C	D	E	F	G
1	Royalty Date	Author Name	Marketplace	Transaction Type	Net Units Sold	Royalty	Currency
2	2021-01-31	Author A	Amazon.com	Standard	0	5.70	USD
3	2021-01-31	Author B	Amazon.com.au	Standard	0	5.03	AUD
4	2021-01-31	Author C	Amazon.com	Free - Price Match	1	0.00	USD
5	2021-01-31	Author D	Amazon.com	Standard	1	2.76	USD
6	2021-01-31	Author C	Amazon.fr	Free - Price Match	1	0.00	EUR
7	2021-01-31	Author C	Amazon.ca	Free - Price Match	1	0.00	CAD
8	2021-01-31	Author A	Amazon.com	Standard	1	5.83	USD
9	2021-01-31	Author C	Amazon.de	Free - Price Match	1	0.00	EUR
10	2021-01-31	Author A	Amazon.com	Standard	1	1.75	USD

Note how the rows are no longer consistently filled or not filled? That's because I "broke" the relationship between Column E and all of the other columns.

To give Excel credit, because I did that with just one column Excel did give a warning, and ask if I wanted to expand my selection. But do that with three or four columns? You're sunk.

This is very, very easy to do, and why you should never work with your raw data. Because you can't fix this later. There's no easy way to reverse a mistake like that once it's made unless you catch it immediately and use Undo (Ctrl + Z) to reverse it.

How To Sort

To sort, first select ALL of the related data for what you need to sort. So all of the rows in your table for a standard sort. This doesn't have to be the full data table, you can just sort a subset, but make sure that you do capture all of the related information to keep from breaking your data.

Next, go to the Sort & Filter dropdown in the Editing section of the Home tab, and choose Custom Sort. (I personally do not use the A to Z and Z to A sort options unless I have just one column of data I'm trying to sort. I want more control over which column is sorted.)

You can also click on the Sort option in the Sort & Filter section of the Data tab, or right-click and go to the secondary dropdown under Sort, and choose Custom Sort from there.

All three will bring up the Sort dialogue box:

The Sort By dropdown is where you can choose which column to sort on. In this particular instance, Excel didn't recognize that I had a header row in the selected cell range, so it by default just shows me Column A, Column B, Column C, etc.

If you do have a header row, click on the checkbox for My Data Has Headers in the top right corner. That will change the list of columns to sort by to use the names from that first row.

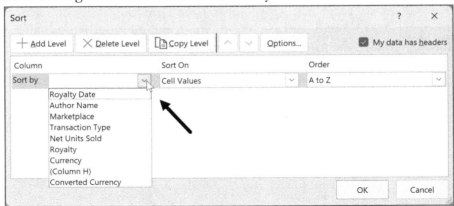

You can also do the reverse, of course, if Excel thinks you have a header row and you don't. Just uncheck the box to see column names instead of values in the first row.

That first level is your primary sort. How would you put these entries together if you were doing so manually. Would you want to look by date, by author, by store, by product type? What's your primary focus?

Choose that in the dropdown.

The next choice is what to sort on. Most of the time it will be the value in the cells. But you can also use this to sort by cell color, font color, or conditional formatting. So if you flag bad entries red and want them all grouped together, you can do that with this dropdown.

Your final choice in that row is how to sort, which will vary based on the type of data and the type of sort, but usually will be ascending or descending.

If you want to then have a secondary sort, click on Add Level and go through those choices for that level. This sort will only happen after the first sort happens. So, for example, if you put date and then author, all of the entries for each date will be grouped together and then within each date the entries will sort by author.

Here I've created a three-level sort:

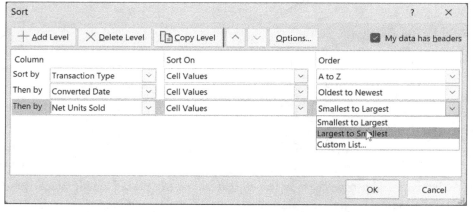

Excel will look at my data and sort it by Transaction Type first, A to Z. Then, within each transaction type, it will sort those entries by date in ascending order from Oldest to Newest. Finally, if there are multiple entries for a specific transaction type on the same day, Excel will sort those entries by number of units sold, in descending order.

Here's what that looks like:

	Royalty Date	Author Name	Marketplace	Transaction Ty	Net Units So	Royalty	Currency		Converted Currency	Converted Date
2	2021-01-26	Author F	Amazon.com	Free - Price Match	1	0.00	USD		$0.00	1/26/2021
3	2021-01-30	Author C	Amazon.com	Free - Price Match	8	0.00	USD		$0.00	1/30/2021
4	2021-01-30	Author F	Amazon.com	Free - Price Match	1	0.00	USD		$0.00	1/30/2021
5	2021-01-30	Author C	Amazon.in	Free - Price Match	1	0.00	INR		$0.00	1/30/2021
6	2021-01-30	Author B	Amazon.com	Free - Price Match	1	0.00	USD		$0.00	1/30/2021
7	2021-01-30	Author C	Amazon.co.uk	Free - Price Match	1	0.00	GBP		$0.00	1/30/2021

The top of my data table now contains all of my free entries, because that is the first transaction type alphabetically. The January 26, 2021 entry is listed first followed by entries for January 30, 2021. Since there are multiple sales on January 30, 2021, the entry that had 8 units "sold" is listed above the ones that had 1 unit sold.

Once you sort data, unless it was already arranged in a specific way that can be replicated, you can't go back to the original order. So sorting is one of those steps you take in Excel that will make a permanent change to your data. Which is fine most of the time, so don't let that scare you out of using it. Just something to be aware of.

A few more tips. To remove a sort level, just bring up the Sort dialogue box, select that line, and then choose Delete Level.

To change the order of the levels you want to sort by, open the Sort dialogue box, click on that line, and then use the up and down arrows at the top of the dialogue box to move that level to where you want it.

Basic Math

There is a lot to learn about how to use formulas and functions in Excel. So much it gets its own books. But I want to quickly cover basic math for you.

See the Sum, Average, and Count

You can just select a cell range with numeric values in it to quickly see the average, count, and sum of those values. The result will display in the bottom right corner of your worksheet.

Right-click in that bottom area to change what will calculations will display.

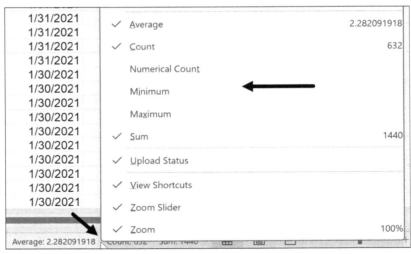

As you can see, your other options are to display calculations of Numerical Count (as opposed to Count which shows the number of cells in the range with something in them), Minimum, or Maximum. Any with a check next to them will display for a selected range of cells. So click on a calculation type to turn it "on" or "off".

Excel will always show Count for selected cells if that option is checked. The other calculations will only show if there are cells in the range that Excel considers numeric, which means dates and/or numbers.

Formulas

To create a formula in Excel, start with an equals sign. Math operators such as the plus sign (+), minus sign (-), division sign (/), and multiplication sign (*) work in Excel. So if you write:

$$=2+3$$

in a cell, that will add 2 to 3 and display a result of 5.
If you write:

$$=2*3$$

in a cell that will multiply 2 times 3 and display a result of 6.

To reference values that are already in cells, just substitute the name of the cells that contain the values. So:

$$=A1+B1$$

will add the values that are in Cells A1 and B1 and display the result.

Those are very basic examples, but Excel can handle extremely complex calculations. If you can write it, Excel will do it. Usually the key is to use your parens to tell Excel which parts of the calculation to do first.

Excel follows standard mathematical rules about calculation order, such as multiplication in a formula before addition. And just like in written math, you can use parens within a formula to control calculation order. A full discussion of the rules Excel follows is under the help topic, Operator Precedence. (See the Learn More chapter to learn about how to use Excel Help.)

Functions

The true power of Excel is in its ability to make calculations that involve many, many cells, which requires using functions.

To use a function, you type the function name, an opening paren, the required information for that function separated by commas, and then a closing paren.

If the formula you're writing only uses that function, then the function comes right after the equal sign that started your formula. Otherwise just include it when it's needed like you would a cell reference or number.

The most basic Excel function is SUM, which adds the values you specify.

Almost every formula you write that uses a function will require cell notation, so let's discuss that now.

Cell Notation

Cell notation is how you tell Excel which cells to include.

To reference a range of cells, use the colon (:) between the first and last cell in the range.

To reference discrete cells or a series of discrete cell ranges, use commas between each cell or cell range.

So if I write:

$$=SUM(A1:C1)$$

That is saying to take the sum of the values in Cells A1 through C1, so Cells A1, B1, and C1. If I write:

$$=SUM(A1, C1)$$

That is saying to take the sum of the values in Cells A1 and C1.

To refer to an entire column you use the letter for that column, a colon, and the letter for that column again (B:B). Same with a row. Number, colon, number. (2:2).

To refer to a range of columns, you use the letter for the first column, a colon, and the letter for the last column. So

$$=SUM(A:E)$$

is saying to sum the values in all rows of Columns A through E.
Same with rows.

$$=SUM(1:5)$$

Is saying to sum the values in all columns of Rows 1 through 5.

When in doubt about how to reference the cells you want to use, start your formula or function, and then select your cells. Excel will write the cell notation for you.

I, for example, never remember how to refer to cells on another worksheet, so I just let Excel do it for me. (The answer is to use the worksheet name with an exclamation point before you list the cell range you want to use from that worksheet. I just go to the worksheet, select the cells, and Excel writes it for me.)

Also, be careful when you write a formula or function that references cells, that you don't accidentally reference the cell you're using to write the formula. That will generate a circular reference error message.

Excel will let you do it, because sometimes people want that, but usually that means you've made a mistake.

Okay. Let's walk through a few more examples.

If you want to subtract all of the values in Column B from the value in Cell A1, you'd write:

$$=A1-SUM(B:B)$$

This is a cheatsheet way to get around the fact that there is no function for subtraction in Excel. When you subtract a series of numbers, you are essentially adding all but the first one together and then subtracting their total from the first value.

$$=7-3-2-1$$

is the same as

$$=7-(3+2+1)$$

To add all of the cells in Columns A and B between Rows 1 and 10, you'd write:

$$=SUM(A1:B10)$$

To add the values in Cells A1, B3, and C6 you'd write:

$$=SUM(A1,B3,C6)$$

To add the cells in Columns A and B between Rows 1 and 10 and Columns E and F between Rows 1 and 10, you'd write:

$$=SUM(A1:B10)+SUM(E1:F10)$$

Or, if you want to be fancy:

$$=SUM(A1:B10,E1:F10)$$

When you write a formula in Excel it will highlight the cells that are being used for the formula. Use this to confirm that you have the right cells selected.

You can also go back to any cell that has a formula in it and double-click on that cell, or click on the cell and use F2, to see what cells are being used and in which part of the formula.

Excel color codes the various components in the formula and uses those same colors for borders it places around the cells used in each component.

AutoSum

One more trick you can use in Excel is the AutoSum option.

Click into the cell at the end of a range of values that you want to add, and then use the AutoSum option in the Editing section of the Home tab. Excel will build the SUM formula for you.

Here I did that in Cell E633 and it wrote a formula that adds six-hundred-and-thirty-one rows of data:

=SUM(E2:E632) ←				
C	D	E	F	G
Amazon.com	Standard - Paperba	1	2.64	USD
Amazon.co.uk	Standard - Paperba	1	4.27	GBP
Amazon.com	Standard - Paperba	1	14.19	USD
Amazon.com	Standard - Paperba	1	4.70	USD
Amazon.com	Standard - Paperba	2	9.16	USD
Amazon.com	Standard - Paperba	1	4.58	USD
Amazon.ca	Standard - Paperba	1	7.95	CAD
Amazon.com	Standard - Paperba	1	14.19	USD
Amazon.com	Standard - Paperba	1	5.40	USD
Amazon.co.uk	Standard - Paperba	1	4.27	GBP
Amazon.com	Standard - Paperba	1	5.75	USD
Amazon.co.uk	Standard - Paperba	1	4.50	GBP
Amazon.com	Standard - Paperba	3	13.74	USD
Amazon.com	Standard - Paperba	1	4.72	USD
Amazon.com	Standard - Paperba	1	5.75	USD
Amazon.com	Standard - Paperba	5	25.80	USD
		=SUM(E2:E632)		
		SUM(**number1**, [number2], ...)		

=SUM(E2:E632)

Pay attention if you use this, though, because it usually stops at any blank cell, so always double-check the formula it writes for you. In the example above it starts with E2, so I know I'm fine, it captured all my entries. But if it were E143, or something like that, I'd know it hadn't captured my full data table, and I'd need to manually adjust the formula.

There are also times when AutoSuml does skip blank cells. I was able to create an example of it here:

tion Type	Net Units Sold	Royalty		Currency	Conver
- Paperba	1	4.70		USD	
- Paperba	2	9.16		USD	
- Paperba	1	4.58		USD	
- Paperba	1	7.95	5.00	CAD	
- Paperba	1	14.19		USD	
- Paperba	1	5.40		USD	
- Paperba	1	4.27		GBP	
- Paperba	1		4.00	USD	
- Paperba	1			GBP	
- Paperba	3	4.27		USD	
- Paperba	1			USD	
- Paperba	1	4.27	6.00	USD	
- Paperba	5	25.80		USD	
	20	=SUM(G13,G9,G5)			
		SUM(number1, [number2], **[number3]**, [number4], ...)			

The formula it wrote is:

$$=SUM(G13,G9,G5)$$

It's nice if you want that, which there have been times I have. For example, I had a table where I was summing every twelve months of results in a column, and wanted a total of those values, but keep an eye on that, too, and make sure that's what you really want it to do.

Another thing to point out is that even though it's called AutoSum, in Excel 2024 you can use the dropdown for AutoSum to calculate the average, count of numbers, maximum, and minimum values.

Just click on the option you want from the dropdown.

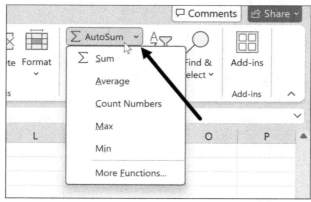

"AutoSum" can also be used to calculate values left to right. So if you want to sum values across a row, just click at the end of the row and then use it.

AutoSum can also be found in the Functions Library section of the Formulas tab.

Other Functions

What we just covered was the down and dirty, very simple version of how to do basic mathematical calculations and use functions in Excel. I've devoted an entire book to this subject, so this was just scratching the surface.

To explore the variety of functions that exist in Excel, click on Insert Function in the Function Library section of the Formulas tab. That will bring up the Insert Function dialogue box where you can click on various function names in the Select a Function section to see a description of what they do.

You can also search in that dialogue box to see if there is a function for the calculation or task you want to perform.

Good functions to explore are SUM, IF or IFS, TEXTJOIN, and XLOOKUP.

Print

Alright, we are almost at the end. The final thing you need to learn as a beginner, is how to print in Excel, which mostly requires learning how to format an Excel worksheet to print well.

To get started, use Ctrl + P or go to the File tab and click on Print from the left-hand menu. Both options will bring up the Print screen:

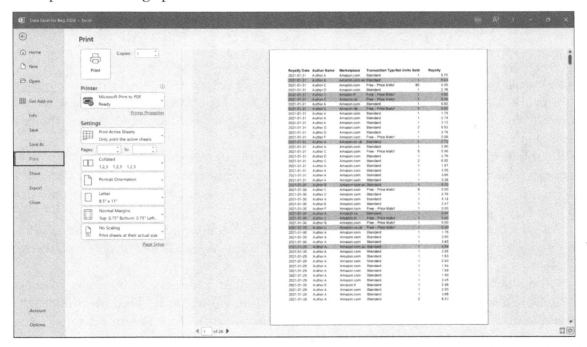

On the right-hand side, you should see a preview of how the first page in the selected worksheet(s) is going to print.

It may not look much like that worksheet.

Note here, for example, that I never put borders around this data, so for print purposes there are no lines on the page to separate columns and rows:

Royalty Date	Author Name	Marketplace	Transaction Type	Net Units Sold	Royalty
2021-01-31	Author A	Amazon.com	Standard	1	5.70
2021-01-31	Author B	Amazon.com.au	Standard	1	5.03
2021-01-31	Author C	Amazon.com	Free - Price Match	65	0.00
2021-01-31	Author D	Amazon.com	Standard	1	2.76
2021-01-31	Author C	Amazon.fr	Free - Price Match	1	0.00
2021-01-31	Author C	Amazon.ca	Free - Price Match	3	0.00
2021-01-31	Author A	Amazon.com	Standard	1	5.83
2021-01-31	Author C	Amazon.de	Free - Price Match	3	0.00
2021-01-31	Author A	Amazon.com	Standard	1	1.75

Also note that there are too many columns to fit on one printed page. I may be able to see all the columns just fine in my worksheet, but that doesn't mean they will print that way. There's also a lot of white space around my actual data.

Below the print preview on the left it will tell you how many pages are going to print:

		2021-01-30	Auth
		2021-01-30	Auth
		2021-01-30	Auth

◄ 1 of 28 ►

Mine currently says 1 of 28 where 28 is the total number of printed pages. To move between your pages, use the arrows on either side of those numbers, enter a value in the white box where it says your current page, or use the scroll bar(s) on the right-hand side of the print preview area.

In this example, my data spreads onto two pages per row because of the number of columns I have. By default Excel goes all the way down the rows before coming back up to the top of the next section, so to see the remainder of my columns for Row 1 I would need to type 15 into that box at the bottom.

Also, by default Excel does not repeat any rows or columns. So page 1 here has a header row and page 15 will have the rest of it, but the rest of the pages will just be data with no clear labels.

On the left of the print preview section is where all of your print options are. These are dynamic and will change depending on the printer you have selected. I keep my printer set to PDF because Office seems to get hung up and slow down when I have it set to my actual printer, which is usually turned off. So before you work with the options there, change it over to the printer you're going to use so you know what options are actually available to you.

Let's walk through that section from top to bottom. Here is a closer look at that options section now that I've switched over to my printer.

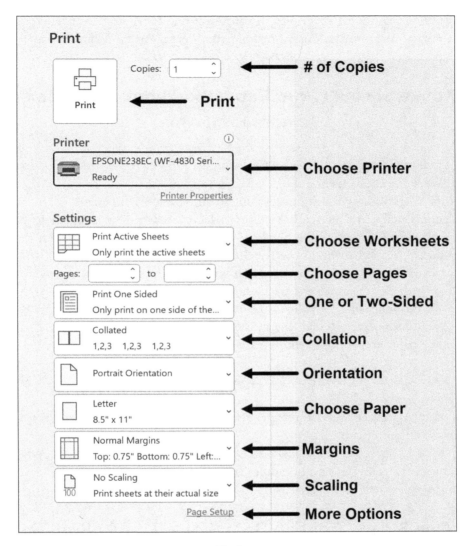

Print

When you're ready to print, click on the print icon there at the top.

Copies

Next to the print icon is an input box for the number of copies to print. The default is 1. You can click on the arrows to move up or down by 1 at a time, or you can just click into the field where it says 1 and type the number you want.

(If you want to print a lot of copies, try printing one copy first to make sure it all looks good before you print more. Making print formatting errors in Excel is just way too common to risk it otherwise.)

Print Active Sheets / Print Entire Workbook / Print Selection / Ignore Print Area

By default, Excel will print the worksheet(s) you currently have selected. The dropdown will show Print Active Sheets for that.

Print Entire Workbook will print everything in all of your worksheets.

Print Selection will print any cells that you selected before you decided to print. If you didn't have any selected, that will be blank. If you just want to print a certain range of cells from a worksheet, this is the one to use for that.

It is possible in Excel to set a print area that will always be the portion of a worksheet that prints. It's like Print Selection except permanent. If you've done that, Print Active Sheets or Print Entire Workbook will only print the cells selected as your print area for that particular worksheet. (We'll discuss how to set that at the end of this chapter.)

To override a print area, choose the Ignore Print Area option.

Pages

If you only want to print some of the pages that you can see in the print preview, it is possible to select a page range to print.

Unlike in Word, this set of pages have to be continuous. The first box there takes the first page you want to print; the second box takes the last.

Your print preview will not change. It will still show all pages that could be printed.

Print One Sided / Print on Both Sides (Long) / Print on Both Sides (Short)

If your printer can do so, you will have the option to print on one side of the page or both sides of the page. The default is one side of the page.

If you choose to print on both sides of the page, you can have it flip on the long side or the short side. In general, I choose long side when printing in portrait orientation and short side when printing in landscape.

Collated / Uncollated

This one only matters if you're printing more than one copy. The choice is between printing all of the first copy, then all of the second copy, then all of the third copy versus printing all copies of page 1, then all copies of page 2, then all copies of page 3.

Collated is when the first copy prints then the second copy, etc. Uncollated is when all of page 1 prints first then all of page 2, etc.

Generally, I choose collated. If I were doing handouts where I handed out each page separately, then I'd do uncollated.

Portrait Orientation / Landscape Orientation

Portrait orientation is when the short edge of the page is across the top and the long edge is down the side. Landscape is when the long edge is across the top and the short edge is down the side.

The default is Portrait Orientation. This is best when you have a limited number of columns and lots of rows. But if you have a large number of columns and want all columns to fit on one page, then Landscape Orientation is the better choice. I often use landscape in Excel.

Letter / Legal / Statement / … / A4 /…

This dropdown is basically asking what paper you're printing on. In the U.S. the default is Letter 8.5" x 11". In other countries it may be A4, which is a standard page size for those countries.

If you need something else, like legal, which will fit more columns in landscape orientation, for example, then choose that paper size from the dropdown. Just be sure that if you're printing to an actual, physical printer that you have that size paper available to print on.

The More Paper Sizes option at the bottom will open the Page Setup dialogue box, but for me the list of choices was the exact same.

Normal Margins / Wide / Narrow / Custom Margins

The next option you have is how much white space you want around the edge of the page. Sometimes if you're very close to fitting all of your information on the page, choosing narrow margins can help, but I tend to leave this one alone.

No Scaling / Fit Sheet on One Page / Fit All Columns on One Page / Fit All Rows on One Page

I use scaling often. It's the easiest way to get all of my information onto one page. So I will use Fit All Columns on One Page if I'm close to getting my data to show on just that one page.

But you have to understand that scaling makes the text smaller to make this happen. And Excel will take you at your word. It will put 50 columns on one page in text so small you can't read it. Or 500 rows on one page.

I often end up using a more advanced scaling option, which we'll discuss under Page Setup.

Page Setup

Clicking on Page Setup launches the Page Setup dialogue box.

It has four tabs: Page, Margins, Header/Footer, and Sheet.

Page Tab

On the Page tab, in the Scaling section, there is an option for Fit To and then two fields that let you specify how many pages wide and how many pages tall you want your printout to be.

Often when I need to scale my data for printing, I will need to do something like 2 pages wide by 3 pages tall, so will use this rather than the scaling dropdown choices available on the Print screen.

Note that 1 wide here would be the same as Fit All Columns on One Page and 1 tall would be the same as Fit All Rows on One Page. This section lets you do both at once, or more than one page for either one or both.

You can also select page orientation and paper source on the Page tab, as well as change the quality of the images you print, but for me at least those options are limited to 300 and 600 dpi.

Margins Tab

The Margins tab I use for Center on Page. I often find when I don't have enough data to fill the printed page, that it looks better if I center my data horizontally.

Header/Footer Tab

The Header/Footer tab has a set of choices for adding a header or footer to each printed page. You can add something as simple as page number or page X of Y. Or you can add something more complex like file name, worksheet name, who prepared the file, date it was printed, etc.

Use the dropdowns that will by default say (none) to choose what you want.

Sheet Tab

The Sheet tab lets you set a print area or set rows or columns to print on every page, but I prefer to do that elsewhere. This tab also lets you choose how pages print so you can have it print across a row and then down columns instead if you want, which is useful if you're printing a range of pages to get the right pages next to each other.

Page Layout Tab

If you go back to your active worksheet and click on the Page Layout tab, you will see in the Page Setup section options for a lot of the print settings we just discussed, such as Margins, Orientation, and Size. They give the same options there as in the print preview screen.

What I use this section for is Print Area and Print Titles.

Print Area

Print Area is where you specify a range of cells on a worksheet that will be all that will print from that worksheet.

This can be useful if you have notes or other data on a worksheet that don't need to print.

To set a print area, select your cells that you want to print, and then click on Set Print Area in the dropdown menu under the Print Area icon.

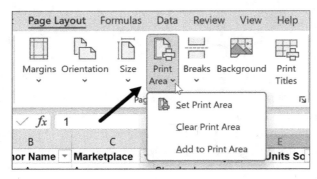

Once you've created a print area, the dropdown will have three choices, Set Print Area, which will override the existing print area you have set, Add to Print Area, which will keep any print area you already set and add the newly selected cells to it, or Clear Print Area, which will remove any selected print area and make it so the whole worksheet prints:

Print Titles

Print Titles lets you tell Excel a series of rows or columns to repeat on every single page that prints.

When you click on Print Titles in the Page Setup section of the Page Layout tab, it will open the Page Setup dialogue box to the Sheet tab.

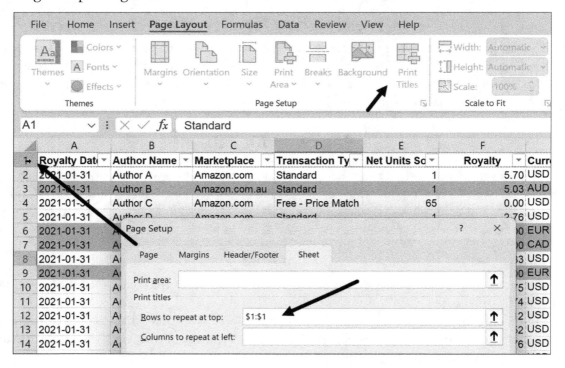

The reason I do this from the actual worksheet instead of the Print screen, is because I can then click into the white cell for Rows to repeat at top, and just click on the 1 for Row 1 to select it. I don't have to remember the cell notation, Excel does it for me.

It is possible to select more than one row or more than one column to repeat on each page.

It is also possible to select a row or column that is not the first row or column.

So if you have some introductory text for a report in Rows 1 through 3 but then the header row is in Row 4, you can just select Row 4.

The only thing you can't do, is select multiple columns or multiple rows that aren't touching. Meaning you can't have Row 1 and 4 repeat. It has to be Rows 1 through 4 or Row 1 or Row 4. Keep that in mind when setting up a report or data table.

Learn More

I can assure you that we have not covered everything you will ever want to know in Microsoft Excel. Guaranteed. But hopefully we covered what you need to know on a day-to-day basis.

If you get deeper into data analysis, then you will highly benefit from learning pivot tables, charts, and functions.

If you want to better flag results, then you should learn conditional formatting.

If you have to mess with data a lot, then it's good to learn how to group data, subtotal it, and use functions.

I of course am biased, and think that if you made it through this book and learned from it, then you should keep going with the rest of this series. The next book is *Intermediate Excel 2024,* which covers conditional formatting, pivot tables, charts, grouping data, subtotaling it, and more. Or you can skip ahead to *Excel 2024 Useful Functions,* to learn more about formulas and functions in Excel.

But. If you, like me, tend to learn better by trial and error, then there are plenty of resources that Microsoft provides to help you learn. (The value I bring is structure around how to approach Excel, and what you can safely ignore.)

So. A few tips for learning on your own:

First, you can hold your cursor over many of the options in the toolbar to see more information about that tool or task.

This will usually tell you what that option does, and give a control shortcut if one exists. Many of them end with Tell Me More. Click on that to be taken to the Excel help specific to that tool or task.

Here, for example, is the Format Painter:

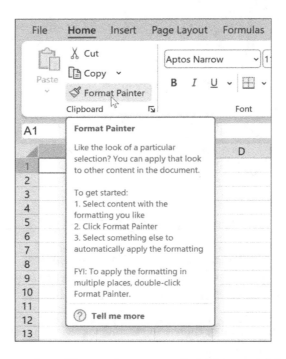

Now, you may be like me, and not like to share every little thing with Microsoft so have turned off all sharing. If that's the case, when you click on Tell Me More, you will get an error message that your administrator has turned this service off.

They haven't. I am my administrator.

What I turned off was "connected experiences". Unfortunately, in Office 2024, rather than let you continue to access Help without being "connected" they force you to choose connected experiences to access it through Excel. (Boo.)

You can turn it back on by going to File and then Options in the bottom left corner. This will bring up the Excel Options dialogue box.

Click on Privacy Settings under General. Scroll down and click the box for "Turn On All Connected Experiences", and then click OK.

You will also need to check the box for Turn On Experiences That Download Online Content. Office will then require you to restart for those changes to take effect. (In my case, I had Skype open, too, and even that is affected. So close anything from Microsoft.)

(Note that if you want to turn these things off, the process is the same, you just uncheck the boxes and restart Office.)

If you don't want that enabled, then use the online search options we'll discuss in a moment.

Okay. So if Help actually works for you, click on that Tell Me More, and Excel will open a task pane on the right-hand side of the screen that lists the help text specific to that task or tool.

Scroll down to read the full text. Click on the X in the top right corner when you're done.

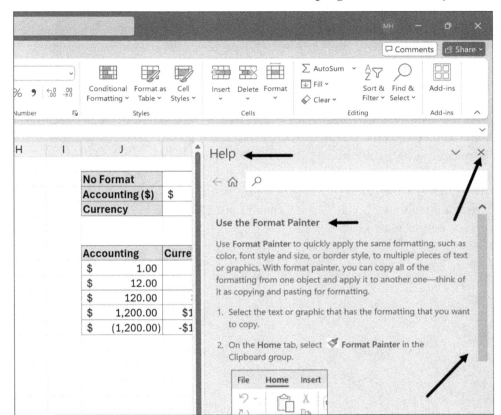

If you want help on something else, you can also use F1, or go to the Help tab and click on Help to open that task pane.

The task pane will open to the main Help page, where you can click on one of the listed topics to learn more, or use the Search box to find the help you need:

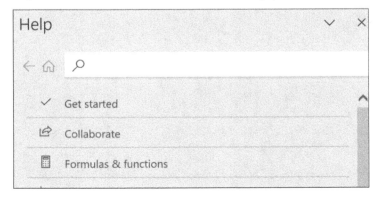

If you go back to the Help tab in the top menu, the Show Training option (which takes a bit to load), has instructional videos you can watch.

The Community and Excel Blog options will take you to websites for each, but honestly once I get away from the help built into Excel, I prefer to do a basic web search.

I type in what I need as well as the version I need it for, so "format painter Excel 2024", and then look for the link to the Microsoft support website (support.microsoft.com).

There are a ton of other free resources out there. YouTube videos are a huge source of information, for example. Just be wary. It's always best to start with the source (Microsoft). I find that they do well at the "how to" guidance, but are less helpful with "can I?".

Also they never cover the pitfalls or pros and cons of various approaches.

Finally, you can always reach out to me if you get stuck. I am happy to help, especially where I didn't cover something in a way that you could follow. (Less so if you try to turn me into your free consultant.) I won't open attachments, though, and I don't always check that email daily, so temper your expectations.

Conclusion

Okay, there you have it. You should be able to work in Excel at this point with some basic data that you can format properly, sort, and filter. You should also be able to do some basic math and navigate around without issues, as well as print your results.

Excel is an incredibly powerful tool. I've been using it for at least 30 years, and I probably only use 20% of its capability. But for most people that's more than they need.

As I mentioned before, this series does continue. If you want to keep going, check out *Intermediate Excel 2024* or *Excel 2024 Useful Functions*.

I also have an older book out there called *Excel for Budgeting* that walks you through how to build an Excel worksheet to use for budgeting purposes, like tracking your spending and income. The companion book for that is *Budgeting for Beginners,* which discusses those concepts. If you don't want to build the actual worksheet, you can just buy a blank template (in .xls format) from my Payhip store. It's linked from my website.

Before we go. You can do this. It may seem daunting, but I have faith in you. Just remember that Ctrl + Z (Undo) or Esc will get you out of almost any misstep you take. You can also just close the file without saving and start over if it's that bad.

And remember to never work directly with your raw data—always keep that set aside for the worst-case scenario.

Take your time.

If you get stuck, remember that Excel is a logical program. Once you learn the structure of it, you should be able to guess how most things are done. Look for the commonalities. (Ctrl + B to bold, Ctrl + I for italics, Ctrl + U to underline, for an example.)

Okay. Good luck with it. Reach out if you get stuck.

Common Control Shortcuts

Task	Ctrl + ...
Bold Text	B
Close File	W
Copy	C
Cut	X
Filter	Shift + L
Go to end of range	[Arrow]
Italicize Text	I
New File	N
Open Find dialogue box	F
Open Replace dialogue box	H
Paste	V
Print Screen (Go To)	P
Redo	Y
Save	S
Select All	A
Select cells in that direction	Shift + [Arrow]
Underline Text	U
Undo	Z

Index

About the Author

M.L. Humphrey is a former stockbroker with a degree in Economics from Stanford and an MBA from Wharton who has spent close to twenty-five years as a regulator and consultant in the financial services industry.

You can reach M.L. at mlhumphreywriter@gmail.com or at mlhumphrey.com.

If you want to buy this book as an ebook, use code EXCEL2024 at https://payhip.com/mlhumphrey to get a fifty percent discount.

www.ingramcontent.com/pod-product-compliance
Lightning Source LLC
LaVergne TN
LVHW081346050326
832903LV00024B/1336